Ann Creber

VINEGARS

Ann Creber

VINEGARS

KEY PORTER · BOOKS

DEDICATION

*For my grandmother, Catherine McLeod
Summers, who first made me aware of kitchen
magic and the lifetime pleasure it imparts, and
for my daughter, Cathie Graham, who now
shares in her great-grandmother's legacy.*

Copyright © 1990 Ann Creber

Canadian Cataloguing in Publication Data

Creber, Ann
  Oils & Vinegars

Canadian ed.
Includes index.
ISBN 1-55013-319-5 (boxed set)
ISBN 1-55013-336-5 (Oils)
ISBN 1-55013-338-1 (Vinegars)

1. Oils and fats, Edible. 2. Vinegar. 3. Cookery
(Vinegar). 4. Cookery. I. Title. II. Title: Oils and vinegars.

TX407.034C74 1991   641.3'385   C91-093260-3

Published in Canada by Key Porter Books Limited,
70 The Esplanade, Toronto, Ontario, M5E 1R2

First published in Australia in 1990 by
CollinsAngus&Robertson Publishers Australia
A division of HarperCollinsPublishers (Australia) Pty Limited
Unit 4, Eden Park, 31 Waterloo Road, North Ryde
NSW 2113, Australia

Printed and bound in Singapore

Contents

ACKNOWLEDGMENTS

I would like to extend thanks to Seppelt & Sons Ltd who provided information about the manufacture of vinegars, and supplied the vinegar I used to produce the various herbal and floral vinegars I created.

Introduction

Vinegar has achieved high status in the fashionable cook's list of ingredients, but its popularity is no new fad: A residue of vinegar in an Egyptian vase proves that the Egyptians were using it in 3000 BC; and vinegar vessels feature in early Greek and Roman drawings. Julius Caesar's armies drank vinegar mixed with water, and Hippocrates prescribed it for his patients. It also appears in the Bible (Book of Ruth 2:14): "And Boaz said unto her, 'At mealtime come though hither and eat of thy bread, and dip the morsel in the vinegar.'" So vinegar is an old friend.

The name vinegar comes from the French words *vin aigre*, meaning sour wine, but it can be made from any liquid that can be turned into alcohol. The process is in two stages: Yeasts convert sugar to alcohol, then bacteria convert alcohol to acetic acid. Although people had been making vinegar for centuries it wasn't until 1864 that Louis Pasteur, the French microbiologist, discovered that it was the bacteria in vinegar that were responsible for converting alcohol to acetic acid. The vinegar bacteria form a thick, sticky skin, which is known as the vinegar mother. Once you have succeeded in growing a vinegar mother (see *page 4*) guard it carefully. It's the vital key to making vinegar at home.

There are many types of vinegar made from many different materials. In southern Europe most vinegar comes from wine, in northern Europe from beer, in the United States from apple cider, and in China and Japan from rice wine. But that's just the start. In the Philippines and Sri Lanka they use coconuts, in Malaysia, pineapples, and in Mexico, cactus leaves. You can learn how to make vinegar from fruit and even how to flavour vinegar with flowers!

Confronted with this range many cooks feel confused. How do you use them? It is important to understand the limitations of each type. For instance, a strongly flavoured malt vinegar would be fine in a robust pickle, but overwhelming in a delicate seafood dish. On the other hand a fine white wine vinegar, which would subtly complement seafood, would be wasted in a pickle. Then there's balsamic vinegar which has its own distinctive flavour and perfume.

I'll explain how the various vinegars are made — and their characteristics and uses — in the following chapters. I'll also tell you how to make your own vinegar. It is a leisurely and absorbing business, which can range from weeks to a year or so, involving a number of variables and the element of chance.

When buying vinegar study the label: It will tell you if the vinegar has been aged properly (if it doesn't provide this information, assume it's an inferior vinegar made by a quick modern process). It should also show the acetic acid content. Wine vinegar is stronger than malt or cider vinegar: Look for wine vinegar with an acetic acid level of at least six percent; and cider or malt with a level of at least four percent. The acetic acid level is important in preserving food — use a commercial vinegar with an acetic acid level of at least four percent, rather than a home-made vinegar with an unknown acetic acid level.

The price range in vinegars is enormous. Be wary of the cheapest: they may be simply water added to acetic acid or they may be commercial vinegars made by quick modern processes, which eliminate the need for ageing in wooden casks. These moderately priced vinegars lack the flavour and aroma of aged vinegars, but are useful for preserving, or can be used when a subtle flavour would be wasted. A good wine vinegar will be comparable with the price of a bottle of wine. A rare balsamic vinegar aged more than 50 years (if you can find one for sale) will cost as much as a fine old Cognac. And vinegar buffs will prize it more!

In the early days vinegar was mainly a condiment, but it was also valued for medicinal purposes. On a recent tour to Israel, I visited a gloomy cellar where prisoners were held at the time of Jesus Christ. The guide told me that two stone jars had been kept near the flogging wall — one contained vinegar, used as an antiseptic, the other oil, used to soothe and heal.

My grandmother, whose Scottish family settled in Australia in the 1840s, always made her own cough mixtures from vinegar and honey. She also used it in hot weather as a "refreshment", dipping a wet handkerchief into a bowl of home-made floral vinegar to dab her forehead, throat, neck, wrists and underarms. In our home we also used it on sunburn, insect stings and nettle rashes.

At one time doctors thought vinegar cured scurvy, believing it was the acid content of citrus fruits (rather than Vitamin C), which helped prevent it. A vinegar ration was issued to sailors on the voyage from England during the early settlement of Australia. It was also given to soldiers with scurvy during the American Civil War.

Vinegar Mother

My first encounter with a vinegar mother was in a dark cupboard in early childhood. My grandmother made many wonderful things in our kitchen, but I was amazed when I discovered a jar filled with a sour-smelling liquid which was covered with a thick, slimy skin. I was poking at it with a large spoon when my grandmother descended upon me to protect her cherished "mother". Now, I have to protect *my* mothers from small granddaughters, who are as intrigued as I was.

What is a vinegar mother? At some stage you have probably thrown one away. Although it is less common nowadays, a vinegar mother sometimes forms on top of a bottle of vinegar which has been unused for some time. The mother first appears as a light veil on the surface. It penetrates the liquid more and more forming a thick folded mat of bacteria (the mycoderma aceti). This micro-organism develops in temperatures between 15°C and 30°C (59°F and 86°F).

How do you make a vinegar mother? There is an element of luck — sometimes it takes off, sometimes it doesn't. Sometimes it's possible to grow a mother on commercial vinegar by exposing it to air. But the following process is the more usual method. Start with some wine or alcoholic apple cider that is free of preservatives — don't use a fortified wine. Pour it into a wide-mouthed crock or dark-coloured glass jar, leaving some room at the top. You can also use a clear glass jar and wrap the sides in foil to keep out the light or you can simply use a bottle containing some left-over wine. Cover the container with muslin or cheesecloth so as to keep out the dust and insects, but to let the air through. Label the container with the starting date and type of wine (if anything special).

When the vinegar mother starts to form (it may take anything from a few weeks to three months or more) you will know that the alcohol is being converted to acetic acid. Wait until the mother resembles a jellyfish, then taste the liquid. If the flavour is weak leave the liquid for another few weeks before tasting it again — it may take six months or more to fully develop. In this time the mother will continue to grow. When there is nothing left for it to live on (when all the alcohol has been converted into acetic acid), it will die if not moved to make a fresh batch of vinegar. When the flavour is satisfactory, strain off the vinegar and bottle (sealing with a cork or ceramic stopper, but not a metal lid which can corrode and affect the flavour).

Use the mother to start another batch or divide it to start several. It's a

good idea to have three batches on the go; white wine, red wine and apple cider. And when handling the mother avoid using metal utensils; they can kill the precious culture.

Of course, if you know someone who already makes their own vinegar, you can make the whole process a lot simpler by begging, borrowing or stealing a piece of a mother. Unfortunately vinegar mothers are not commercially available.

Wine Vinegar

In the Middle Ages, vinegar was the great hazard of the wine trade. It didn't take long for some wine-makers to realize that they could turn their bad luck to good account. In 1394 they established a guild of professional vinegar makers, the Corporatif des Maîtres-Vinaigriers d'Orléans, in Orléans, one of the major centers of the French wine trade.

The best wine vinegars are still made using the old Orléans process. Oak barrels, three-quarters filled with wine, are laid on their sides, with small air holes drilled in the top. The temperature is maintained at about 21°C (70°F). A vinegar mother forms on the surface turning the alcohol into acetic acid which moves to the bottom of the cask. Vinegar can then be drawn off from the bottom of the cask and more wine can be added to replace it.

Wine vinegars made by this slow, natural process are expensive, but represent good value. Study the label of a bottle of vinegar. If vinegar has been properly aged it will indicate Made by the Orléans Process, Aged in Wood, or Vinaigre à l'Ancienne.

Cheap commercial wine vinegars are mostly made by mechanically dripping wine through casks loosely packed with wood shavings to provide a surface for the wine to be exposed to air, so that bacteria can proliferate and turn the alcohol into acetic acid. Submerged fermentation, another modern method, involves mechanically dispersing air bubbles through the wine. Both these quick processes drive off volatile aromas. The slow method of making vinegar uses a limited amount of air, so retaining the flavour and aroma. Quick method vinegars are fine for some recipes, but can't compare with vinegars that have matured slowly and naturally.

If you are making your own vinegar it's worth starting with a respectable wine: The best wine makes the best vinegar. Don't mix red with white and don't start with a mixture of the dregs of wine and expect to produce a fine vinegar — hit and miss methods sometimes make very good vinegar, but more often the result is raw and coarse. You will need a vinegar mother; if you don't have one, use the method described on *page 4*. If you already have a vinegar mother simply pour the wine into a crock or dark-coloured glass jar, add the mother, and cover with muslin or cheesecloth. Leave it in a dark cupboard for a few weeks before tasting. If the flavour is right, strain and bottle the vinegar, otherwise leave it for another few weeks and try again. It can take six months or more for the flavour to fully develop.

Good wine vinegar is clear, and if made from white wine, it is pale gold, almost colourless; if made from red wine, it is pink and is always lighter than the original wine. The taste is distinctly acidic, and the aroma is reminiscent of the wine from which it comes.

Commonsense will tell you when to use a fine wine vinegar and when it would be wasted. In a salad, for instance, where the vinegar adds its separate and distinct flavour without overwhelming or being overwhelmed, quality is important. On the other hand you wouldn't waste a fine wine vinegar on pickling onions or anything else with a strong flavour.

WHITE WINE VINEGAR

Pickled · Onions

No book on vinegars would be complete without a recipe for pickled onions! This method ensures crisp-textured onions.

1 kg (2.2 lb) small white onions, peeled
About 30g (1 oz) coarse salt
1 l (32 fl oz) white wine vinegar

2 teaspoons black peppercorns
1 teaspoon mustard seeds
3 to 4 whole cloves
1 bay leaf

Place the onions in a stainless steel, glass or pottery bowl and sprinkle with the salt. Allow to stand overnight.

Next day, rinse the salt off the onions; place them into a colander to drain. In a non-reactive saucepan, boil the vinegar with the peppercorns, mustard seeds, cloves and bay leaf for 10 to 15 minutes. Add the onions and boil for no more than 5 minutes.

Pack the onions into small sterilised jars. Pour on the vinegar, discarding the cloves. The other spices may be added to the jars to enhance the appearance. Set aside to cool completely. Seal the jars. Store in a cool place, away from light for at least 1 week to allow the flavours to blend and mellow.

Makes about four 250g (8 oz) jars

NOTE: Cider vinegar may be substituted for the white wine vinegar.

Pickled · Eggs

Pickled eggs are delicious as part of a smorgasbord, as a satisfying low-kilojoule (calorie) snack or as part of a ploughman's lunch, served with good bread, cheese, pickled onions and maybe a slice or two of ham.

My grandmother used a rather fierce malt vinegar for her pickled eggs. I use a gentler white wine vinegar — try cider vinegar for a change, it provides a good base.

12 small hard-boiled eggs, peeled	1 tablespoon black peppercorns
	2 to 3 large thyme sprigs
1 l (32 fl oz) white wine vinegar	1 small garlic clove, slivered (optional)
2 bay leaves	2 whole cloves

Place the eggs in a large wide-mouthed jar. In a non-reactive saucepan, combine the vinegar, bay leaves, peppercorns, thyme sprigs, garlic and cloves. Bring to a boil; reduce the heat and simmer for about 15 minutes.

Allow to cool a little. Pour the vinegar, with the herbs and spices, over the eggs, ensuring they are well covered. (If necessary, add a little water.) Set aside to cool completely. Cover the jar, but don't use a metal lid. These eggs keep very well for several weeks (at least!) without needing refrigeration.

Makes 1 dozen

Pickled · Octopus

I recently ate this dish in Athens and although I have enjoyed it before, I found this version particularly delectable. It's not everybody's favourite, I admit, but do try it.

1 medium octopus (about 1 kg; 2 lb) or squid	½ cup (4 fl oz) white wine vinegar
3 tablespoons dry white wine	½ teaspoon salt
	Plenty of pepper
1½ garlic cloves, finely slivered	Good squeeze lemon juice
½ cup (4 fl oz) virgin olive oil	Continental (flatleaf) parsley

Clean the octopus by removing the intestines and ink sac. Discard the sac — we don't use it in this recipe. Remove the eyes and beak, pull off the skin and rinse well. Remove the tentacles. Place the cleaned head and tentacles into a pan with a few tablespoons of white wine. Cover the pan and simmer the octopus with the wine and its own juices for about 45 minutes, or until the octopus is tender and rosy in colour. Drain and allow to cool.

Cut the octopus flesh and tentacles into small pieces and place in a bowl. Add the garlic, oil, vinegar, salt and pepper. Toss well, cover and set aside to marinate for at least 15 hours. Stir occasionally.

To serve, remove the octopus pieces from the liquid, drain lightly and spoon onto a serving dish. Squeeze on lemon juice and garnish with the parsley leaves. Serve with a selection of pickled vegetables, olives, spicy sausages, cheese and coarse-textured breads, and a carafe of white wine, and you have a feast fit for Apollo himself!

Serves 6 to 8

Pickled · Walnuts

Let's face it, preparing your own pickled walnuts is a bit fiddly. It also ruins your hands for weeks unless you wear rubber gloves! However, you'll agree it is worth the effort when you see the price of the small jars of these delicacies in gourmet stores. It is vital to choose walnuts that are still green and soft skinned, otherwise the results will be disappointing.

10 cups (2½ l; 80 fl oz)   *green, soft-shelled walnuts*
water mixed with 250 g   *5 cups (1¼ l; 40 fl oz)*
(8 oz) coarse salt   *white wine vinegar*
2 kg (about 4½ lb) small,

Wearing rubber gloves, prick the walnuts all over with a darning needle (if the needle will not penetrate, the walnuts are too mature to pickle. Place the walnuts in a glass or ceramic bowl and pour on the salt water mixture. Cover with a cloth. Place a weighted plate on top to ensure all walnuts are covered. Set aside for 5 days in a cool place. Drain off the soaking solution. Make another brine solution and pour over walnuts. Repeat the above procedure and allow to stand for a further 7 days. Drain well.

Spread the nuts onto paper-covered trays. Let air dry, turning from time to time, for 24 hours, or until the skins turn black. Fill bottles with walnuts, leaving a little space at the top of each bottle.

Pour on vinegar to cover the walnuts. Cover with plastic wrap and a plastic lid. Set aside for 10 days before using.

Makes about two 500 g (16 oz) jars

Preserved · Capsicums (Bell Peppers)

This offers a wonderful way of allowing us to enjoy summer's harvest in the dark days of winter. I serve strips of preserved capsicum as part of a simple antipasto or to add depth of flavour to a rice salad.

6 large, very ripe red or yellow capsicums (bell peppers)

½ cup (approximately 20 leaves) fresh basil leaves
White wine vinegar
Olive oil

Cut the capsicums in half lengthwise; remove the seeds. Char them over an open flame or under a hot grill until the skin blackens and blisters all over. Place into a plastic bag, seal firmly and allow to stand for about 20 minutes. Peel off the skins. Set aside to cool.

Pack the capsicums in layers in a preserving jar, arranging several basil leaves between each layer. Cover with white wine vinegar and pour a thin layer of olive oil on top to seal.

To serve, drain well and cut the peppers into strips or chunks. Sprinkle with lots of black pepper and a little olive oil or serve as suggested above.

Makes about two 500 g (16 oz) jars

Preserved · Horseradish · in · Vinegar

I always seem to have a super-abundance of horseradish in my herb garden and it is not an ingredient that can be used every day! I find this is a good way of preserving it for those occasions when I really do need it for a recipe.

Young horseradish roots	Sugar
(old ones become too	Fresh red chilies
woody and fiercely hot)	White wine vinegar
Salt	

Wash and peel the horseradish roots, grate immediately. (To prevent a lot of weeping, I suggest you use the grater attachment on your food processor.)

Spoon the horseradish into a small jar, filling each about two-thirds full. Add ½ teaspoon salt and ½ teaspoon sugar to each jar and stir into the horseradish. Add a small sliver of red chili to each jar. Fill the jars with the vinegar. Cover with paper, and screw each lid firmly into place.

To use, strain off the vinegar and rinse the horseradish to remove the vinegary flavour. Press out as much liquid as possible. The vinegar may be used to add zip to salad dressings!

Horseradish Cream

2 tablespoons drained	1 teaspoon castor
preserved horseradish	(granulated) sugar
(see recipe, above	Freshly ground black
1 teaspoon white wine	pepper
vinegar	¾ cup (6 fl oz) heavy
1 teaspoon dry mustard	cream

In a bowl, mix together the drained horseradish, vinegar, mustard, sugar and pepper. Blend thoroughly. Lightly whip the cream. Fold in the horseradish mixture. Serve with cold meats; this sauce is especially good with roast beef, either cold or hot.

Makes about 1 cup (8 fl oz)

Bishops' · Bread

This is an old recipe, the origin of which I can't find. It is interesting to note how many old-fashioned cake and biscuit recipes used vinegar as an ingredient, often as a "lightening" agent.

2½ cups (10 oz) sifted plain (all-purpose) flour
1¾ cups (9 oz) firmly packed brown sugar
½ cup (2 oz) butter or margarine
1 teaspoon baking powder

1 teaspoon bicarbonate of soda (baking soda)
1 teaspoon ground cinnamon
1 tablespoon white wine vinegar
¾ cup (6 fl oz) milk
1 large egg

Combine flour and sugar in a large bowl. Work in the shortening using two knives, a pastry blender or your fingertips until the mixture is the consistency of crumbs. Set aside ¾ cup (3 oz) of the mixture for topping. Add the baking powder, bicarbonate of soda and cinnamon and mix well.

Stir in the milk, vinegar and egg. Mix with a hand-held electric beater until smooth. Pour the mixture into a buttered baking tin approximately 25 x 30 cm (10 x 12 inches) and spread evenly. Sprinkle reserved topping evenly over the surface.

Bake in a preheated 190 °C (375 °F) oven for about 25 minutes or until golden brown and just firm to the touch. Cool in the tin, before cutting into squares. Serve warm or at room temperature.

Makes 20

RED WINE VINEGAR

Tomato · Juice · Cocktail

600 ml (20 fl oz) tomato
juice, well chilled
1 small white onion, finely
chopped or grated
1 tablespoon red wine
vinegar

1 tablespoon brown sugar
½ teaspoon garlic salt
2 tablespoons chopped
basil leaves
Freshly grated pepper
Lemon wedges

Combine all of the ingredients except lemon wedges in a large jug; mix well. Allow to chill for 1 hour. Strain and pour into frosty cold glasses. Garnish with a lemon wedge on each glass rim.

Serves 4 to 6

Kiopoolu
(Bulgarian Aubergine (Eggplant) Spread)

This robust-flavoured spread is a good choice to serve either with dark breads, crispbread or vegetable crudités. It may be made up a day or so before it is required.

750 g (1½ lb) aubergine
(eggplant)
2 small red or green
capsicums (bell peppers)
3 tablespoons olive oil
3 tablespoons red wine
vinegar
1 ripe tomato, peeled and
seeded

2 tablespoons finely
chopped parsley
2 garlic cloves, minced
Pepper, to taste
Vegetable salt (optional)
Strips of tomato and red or
green capsicum (bell
peppers), for garnish

Prick the aubergine skin in several places. Place it on baking sheet and broil under a hot griller, turning until the skin is blackened, about 20 minutes.

Wrap the aubergine in a damp teatowel for about 5 minutes. Unwrap and peel off the skin. Cut the aubergine in half; chop flesh very finely. Mash the flesh to a pulp. (It may be put through a food mill or lightly processed in a food processor.)

Cut the capsicums in half; discard membranes and seeds. Capsicums may also be grilled (broiled) first, if preferred. Finely chop the peppers mash to a pulp. Combine with the aubergine pulp. Gradually add the oil and vinegar and stir in.

Combine the tomato with the parsley, garlic and pepper and salt. Stir into the aubergine mixture. Blend thoroughly. Cover and chill well. Serve garnished with strips of tomato and capsicum.

Serves 6 to 8

Mussels · Vinaigrette

I love mussels, and find this an excellent way to serve them. I remember eating mussels at a tiny restaurant in the French town of Angers; I was alone and counted the huge pile I was served. There were 54 — but I should add that the largest shell was little larger than the size of my thumb nail, while the smallest was no bigger than my little finger nail! You will probably have to settle for the local variety, but served this way they will be delicious.

¼ cup (2 fl oz) dry white wine

2 garlic cloves, crushed

750 g (1½ lb) mussels, scrubbed and debearded

¾ cup (6 fl oz) vegetable oil

¼ cup (2 fl oz) red wine vinegar

2 teaspoons Dijon mustard

Freshly ground pepper

Mixed lettuce leaves

1 avocado, sliced, chopped and brushed with lemon juice

1 cup (16 whole) cherry tomatoes, halved

8 small spring onions (scallions), finely chopped

Combine the wine and garlic in a large non-reactive saucepan. Place a steamer in the pan and add sufficient water to come to just below the base of the steamer. Bring to a boil. Place the unopened mussels in the steamer. Cover and steam for about 3 minutes. Remove the opened mussels and cook the remainder for a further 3 minutes. (Discard any that do not open after that time.) Transfer the mussels to a bowl; cover and chill for several hours.

To make the vinaigrette: In a bowl, whisk together the oil, vinegar, mustard and pepper.

Arrange the lettuce leaves on a platter. Top with the mussels and sprinkle on the chopped avocado, cherry tomatoes and the chopped spring onions. Pour on the vinaigrette. Serve with plenty of bread.

Serves 4

Roast · Filet · of · Beef · with Red · Wine · and · Peppercorn · Sauce

Choose a well-shaped whole filet for this dish and trim it neatly to shape.

2 tablespoons melted butter	6 tablespoons coarsely crushed black peppercorns
1¼ kg (about 2½ lb) whole eye filet or 2 smaller filets of beef	2 garlic cloves, slivered

Sauce

90 g (3 oz) shallots (scallions) or small pickling onions	3 tablespoons jellied veal stock
1 bottle dry red wine	About 250 g (8 oz) butter
1 small bay leaf	About 2 tablespoons red wine vinegar
1 thyme sprig	

Trim the filet to a neat shape, discarding sinews and excess fat. Heat the butter in a baking dish and brown the filet all over. Make a number of slits in the meat with the tip of a small knife; insert small pieces of the garlic. Press the crushed peppercorns onto the surface of the meat.

Roast the filet in a preheated moderate 180°C (350 °F) oven for about 35 minutes. (Test for preferred colour of meat.)

Prepare the sauce: Combine the shallots and red wine in a non-reactive saucepan. Simmer until reduced to about ¾ cup. Add the veal stock (which should be of a jellied consistency) and continue reducing until sauce is of a syrupy consistency.

Whisk in small pieces of butter as for a butter sauce. Do not allow the sauce to become melted; the sauce should actually thicken as the butter is whisked in. Add the vinegar in small quantities until the flavour of the sauce is slightly acidic.

To serve, cut the beef into slices. Spoon on some of the sauce or serve separately in a jug or gravy boat.

Serves 6

Braised · Okra · and · Aubergine (Eggplant)

Both of these vegetables are very familiar in Middle Eastern and Greek cooking, but are still somewhat neglected elsewhere. Try this interesting vegetable dish when okra (also known as lady's fingers) is briefly available in the shops.

*500g (1 lb) fresh okra
(lady's fingers)
½ cup (4 fl oz) red wine
vinegar
500g (1 lb) small
aubergines (eggplants)
Salt
1 large onion, thinly sliced
2 garlic cloves, finely
chopped*

*½ cup (4 fl oz) olive oil
2 cups (12 oz) chopped,
peeled ripe tomatoes
(canned tomatoes may be
used)
2 tablespoons finely
chopped parsley
¾ teaspoon sugar
Freshly ground pepper*

Wash the okra and trim stalks. Place the okra in a bowl, pour over the vinegar and allow to stand for about 30 minutes.

Cut the aubergines into slices or, if using larger aubergine, cut into cubes. Place the sliced aubergine into a colander, sprinkle with salt and allow to drain for about 30 minutes. After that time, rinse well and pat dry.

Gently fry the onion and garlic in the heated olive oil until the onion softens. Pat dry the drained okra and add to the onion and garlic. Cook until lightly coloured. Add the sliced aubergine and lightly brown on each side.

Add the remaining ingredients, adjusting the quantity of sugar and pepper to taste. Cover and simmer gently for about 30 minutes, or until the vegetables are tender. To serve, sprinkle with additional finely chopped parsley. This is very good served with spit-roasted lamb.

Serves 6

Christmas · Eve · Salad

I discovered this colourful and delicious recipe several years ago when I was researching a Mexican cookbook. Traditionally served in Mexico on Christmas Eve, it usually accompanies Chicken or Turkey Molé, the famous Mexican dish that features a chocolate-flavoured sauce.

1 crisp, firm head of lettuce, shredded
3 oranges, peeled and segmented
2 firm bananas, peeled, sliced and brushed with lemon juice or vinegar
1 large apple, unpeeled, but cored and sliced (brush with lemon or vinegar)

1 cup (6 oz) fresh pineapple chunks
1 cup (6 oz) sliced cooked beetroot
½ cup (3 oz) coarsely chopped toasted peanuts
Seeds of 1 pomegranate, if available

Red Wine Vinegar Dressing

¼ cup (2 fl oz) red wine vinegar
1 tablespoon water
1 tablespoon sugar

½ teaspoon sweet paprika	*or 1 teaspoon chopped*
½ teaspoon dried mustard	*fresh tarragon*
½ teaspoon celery seed	*Freshly ground pepper*
½ garlic clove	*⅔ cup (5 fl oz) vegetable*
½ teaspoon dried tarragon	*oil*

Shred the lettuce onto a serving platter. Arrange the oranges, bananas, apple, pineapple and beets attractively on the lettuce. Sprinkle on the peanuts and pomegranate seeds.

Make the dressing by combining the vinegar, water, sugar, paprika, mustard, celery seed, garlic, tarragon and pepper in a jar. Shake vigorously. Add the oil and shake until completely blended.

Pour as much dressing as required over the salad and serve at once. Cover and chill any leftover dressing for later use.

Serves 8 to 10

Broccoli · Salad · with · Grainy
Mustard · Dressing

I prefer to serve this salad at room temperature, rather than chilled. It looks attractive and tastes terrific!

500g (1 lb) broccoli, cut	*⅓ cup (2½ fl oz) extra-*
into bite-size florets	*light olive oil*
1 large red capsicum (bell	*2 tablespoons red wine vinegar*
pepper), cut into julienne	*1 tablespoon coarse-*
½ cup (8 whole) cherry	*grained mustard*
tomatoes, halved	*Black pepper*

Bring a large saucepan of lightly salted water to a boil. Add the broccoli and boil for 2 minutes. Cool quickly under cold running water. Set aside. Toss the broccoli, capsicum julienne and cherry tomatoes together in a salad bowl. Combine the dressing ingredients in a bowl and whisk until well blended. (Alternatively, combine dressing ingredients in a sealed jar and shake well.) Pour the dressing over the salad and toss to coat well. Serve at once.

Serves 6

Chili · Sauce

Serve this robust sauce with any meats that call for a hot and spicy accompaniment. Good for barbecued meats.

3 large tomatoes, peeled
   and quartered
1 tablespoon chili powder
   (use a mild chili powder
   or adapt quantity to
   taste)
2 teaspoons dry mustard
2 teaspoons horseradish
   sauce

½ teaspoon sugar
1 teaspoon curry powder
1 onion, chopped
1 garlic clove, chopped
Large pinch of cayenne
   pepper
¼ cup (2 fl oz) red wine
   vinegar

Combine all of the ingredients in a large non-reactive saucepan; mix well. Simmer until tender and well flavoured, adding a little water during the cooking, if necessary. Pass the sauce through a sieve or purée in a blender. Refrigerate for a week or more.

Makes about 1½ cups (12 fl oz)

Zesty · Hawaiian · Dressing

Use this to add interest to almost any salad. It is particularly good when served with salads that accompany rich meats, such as duck.

6 tablespoons red wine vinegar	⅓ teaspoon Tabasco sauce
3 tablespoons water	¼ teaspoon celery seed
2 tablespoons lemon juice	½ garlic clove, finely chopped
2 tablespoons pineapple juice	⅓ cup (2½ fl oz) vegetable oil
¼ cup (3 oz) honey	Freshly ground black pepper
½ teaspoon sweet paprika	

Combine the vinegar, water and juices and stir well. Stir in the honey, paprika, Tabasco, celery seed and garlic. Whisk in the oil and pepper. Cover and chill the dressing for several hours or overnight to allow the flavours to blend and mellow.

Makes about 1 cup (8 fl oz)

Balsamic Vinegar

Balsamic vinegar is the Rolls Royce of vinegars. Perhaps it sounds ridiculous to describe a vinegar as romantic, but for me the whole concept and tradition of this beautiful vinegar, which comes from the province of Modena in Italy, is just that.

It has been made since the Middle Ages and it was then thought to possess medicinal properties, hence its name balsamico — a balsam. In 1046 a barrel of it was among coronation gifts to the Holy Roman Emperor Henry III. With its sweet-sour flavour, rich brown colour and intensely aromatic fragrance it is a gift fit for kings and is quite different to other vinegars — even other fine wine vinegars.

Balsamic vinegar is made from grapes with a high sugar content, such as trebbiano, lambrusco and salamino. The juices are boiled down to make a syrup which is cooled and transferred to a barrel, where it is exposed to yeasts in the air. These yeasts turn some of the sugar into alcohol, but because of the initial high sugar content, a residue of sugar remains. The vinegar is then aged at least three years.

In fact, home-made balsamic vinegars are often aged over several generations of a family. After ten years or more, when much of the content of the original barrel has evaporated (and the flavour has intensified), the remainder is poured into a smaller barrel. After another decade or so, as evaporation continues, the vinegar, now even more intense in flavour, is poured into a smaller cask. And so it continues, from generation to generation. When it reaches the final, acceptable reduction, the precious essence is sealed in a final small wooden cask.

The oldest balsamic vinegars — from fifty to more than 200 years old — are among the world's most expensive foods, rivalling even caviar, truffles and old cognac. When Modena was bombed during World War II, families saved their barrels of balsamic vinegar ahead of other precious possessions.

Balsamic vinegars are still made at home by Modenese families, but the very old balsamic vinegars are rarely sold. They are kept for family use, given to daughters as part of their dowries or passed on as heirlooms.

Commercial manufacturers now produce it in considerably less time, although to be labelled *aceto balsamico*, Italian law requires that it must age a minimum of three years in a wooden cask made of juniper, oak, chestnut or mulberry. It is still a fine product and is still expensive, but it can be used sparingly to create its magic.

A few drops added to a pan for deglazing makes a great difference to the flavour of a sauce and even a small amount transforms a dressing. You can use it alone on salads and also as a cordial — add a dash to a glass of soda water. Buy one bottle of the best you can afford and treat it like liquid gold, but also invest in a cheaper one which you can use more lavishly. And please, when you use balsamic vinegar, think of the history, tradition, and — yes — romance that created it.

Chilled · Canteloupe · and · Peach · Soup

Cool and fragrantly delicious, this summer-day soup is "sparked" by the addition of a little balsamic vinegar. To ensure you choose a perfectly ripe canteloupe, sniff its rough surface — the fragrance of luscious melon should delight your nose.

1 medium canteloupe (rockmelon)
3 large very ripe yellow peaches
1/3 cup (2 1/2 fl oz) fresh orange juice
2 teaspoons sugar
2 drops of chili sauce (see recipe, page 21)
White pepper

1 tablespoon balsamic vinegar
1 tablespoon very finely chopped mint (eau de cologne mint adds even more fragrance)
Shreds of orange peel, for garnish
A few whole mint leaves, for garnish

Halve the melon; scoop out seeds and membranes, reserving any juice. Spoon the flesh into a blender or food processor; lightly purée.

Peel the peaches; cut into small pieces and add to the melon together with the orange juice and sugar. Process until silken-smooth; pour into a bowl. Season with chili sauce and pepper. Cover and chill for about 1 hour.

Stir in the vinegar and mint. Ladle the soup into chilled bowls. Garnish each with a few shreds of orange peel and mint leaves.

Serves 6

Fragrant · Smoked · Chicken · Salad

This is a wonderful salad to serve as a light first course. Serve with a generous portion of interesting greens for maximum effect.

1 large grapefruit
3 tablespoons balsamic
  vinegar

1 teaspoon shredded fresh
  basil
½ teaspoon finely chopped
  marjoram

Freshly ground pepper
½ cup (4 fl oz) extra-
   virgin olive oil
4 cups (8 oz) mixed salad
   greens such as a variety
   of lettuce leaves, rocket,
   endive, cress, etc.

500 (1 lb) smoked chicken
   or turkey, thinly sliced
1 avocado, peeled, sliced
   and brushed with lemon
   juice
Warm toasted almonds

Carefully remove all of the peel and pith from the grapefruit; cut the flesh into segments from between the membranes. Place in a small bowl.

Combine the vinegar, herbs and pepper in a bowl. Gradually pour in the oil, whisking constantly.

Combine well washed, dried, crisp greens and mix together. Pour on about one-third of the dressing and toss lightly.

Arrange the greens, grapefruit segments, chicken and avocado slices alternately on one large plate or individual plates. Sprinkle with the remaining dressing. Top with toasted almonds and serve at once.

Serves 6

NOTE: If you can track down a delicious and mild flavoured pink grapefruit, this recipe is even more fragrant and delicious.

Strawberries · With · a · Splash

For a delectable and refreshing summer dessert, serve strawberries with the fragant and palate-tingling addition of balsamic vinegar. Popular in Italy, it offers an interesting change from the inevitable strawberries and cream.

500 g (1 lb) small ripe
   strawberries
1 to 2 tablespoons castor
   (granulated) sugar

2 tablespoons balsamic
   vinegar
Almond bread wafers

Hull the strawberries and wipe each with a damp cloth. (Cultivated berries seldom need more than a wipe.) Place them into a shallow bowl. Sprinkle on the sugar and the balsamic vinegar. Chill for 1 hour.

Spoon into small serving plates and serve with almond bread. Pass additional sugar separately for those with a sweet tooth.

Serves 4

Sweet · Onion · Marmalade

Serve this delectable relish with cold meats or cheese — it offers a delightful change from conventional pickles.

¼ cup (2 fl oz) olive oil
1 kg (2 lb) onions, cut into thin slices from top to base
2 tablespoons raw sugar (brown sugar)
½ teaspoon freshly ground black pepper
¼ teaspoon ground cloves
¼ teaspoon ground allspice
¼ cup (2 fl oz) balsamic vinegar
¼ cup (2 fl oz) light chicken stock
Salt

Heat the oil gently in a large pan over moderate heat. Add the onions and cook until softened, stirring often, about 15 minutes.

Add the sugar, pepper and spices. Cook for 10 minutes, stirring frequently. Add the vinegar and cook for 5 minutes, stirring from time to time. Add the stock; reduce the heat to low. Cover and cook, stirring occasionally, for 35 minutes or so. Add more pepper if needed and a little salt, if desired.

Cover and chill until required.

Makes about two 250 g (8 oz) jars

NOTE: This may be made 4 to 5 days in advance.

Sherry Vinegar

Sherry vinegar is made around Jerez in the southwestern area of Spain. Its flavour is mellow and full-bodied, a little like balsamic vinegar, and although it is excellent for dressings, I particularly like it in dishes that contain sugar or honey. Usually available only as a gourmet line in specialty shops, it is, not surprisingly, expensive: The best sherry vinegars are aged for twenty to thirty years before bottling.

In most recipes calling for sherry vinegar, you can substitute white wine vinegar, or blend one-third sherry vinegar with two-thirds white wine vinegar.

Chicken · Breasts · in · Mustard · Summer Fruits

Adapted from a traditional Italian recipe that uses candied fruits in a mustard syrup, this version relies on home-preserved seasonal fruits. The flavours of the chicken and fruits, combined with the tangy mustard syrup, offer a delight for the palate.

500 g (1 lb) mixed summer fruits such as	*plums, apricots, figs, kumquats, firm yellow peaches*

300 g (6 oz) white (castor or granulated) sugar
¾ cup (6 fl oz) water
3 tablespoons sherry vinegar (use cider vinegar or white wine vinegar, if necessary)

2 tablespoons yellow mustard seeds
2 whole cloves
4 whole boneless chicken breasts, skin removed
Salt (optional)
Black pepper

To prepare the fruit preserve: remove the stones (where necessary). Cut the fruit into quarters and place in a bowl.

Combine the sugar and water in a saucepan. Heat gently, stirring occasionally, until the sugar dissolves. Bring to the boil, reduce the heat and cook gently without stirring for 10 minutes.

Set aside to cool. Stir in the vinegar, mustard seeds and cloves. Pour onto the fruits, mix very gently and spoon into a wide-necked jar. Seal and refrigerate for at least 1 week before using.

To cook the chicken: Sprinkle each chicken breast with a little salt and pepper. Lightly butter four squares of foil. Place a chicken breast onto each. Spoon on a small quantity of the mustard fruit preserves. Loosely fold over the foil to form a packet.

Arrange the pockets on a shallow baking tray. Bake in a preheated moderate (180°; 350° F) oven for about 30 minutes, or until cooked as preferred.

Remove the chicken from the foil, place on serving plates. (I prefer to serve this dish warm, rather than hot.) Pass the remaining mustard fruit preserve separately. Serve a delicate salad composed of pretty baby greens.

Serves 4

NOTE: This mustard fruit sauce is excellent with cold lamb, poultry or ham.

Champagne Vinegar

"Champagne" vinegar is a nice idea, but the somewhat disappointing truth is that the champagne vinegar you buy isn't made from champagne. It comes from still dry white wine — an ideal wine for making vinegar — grown in the Champagne district of France. But you can make your own vinegar from leftover champagne.

Spring · Vegetable · Terrine · with Champagne · Dressing

A light first course or, in large portions, an ideal main course for the first warm days — it takes advantage of the tiny spring vegetables which begin to appear in gardens and shops at that time.

2 baby leeks, trimmed and
  well washed
2 baby zucchini
  (courgettes)
2 baby carrots
6 small asparagus spears
4 spring onions (scallions)
5 to 8 spinach leaves,
  blanched

1 tablespoon finely
  chopped chervil
4 whole eggs
2 egg yolks
1½ cups (12 fl oz) milk
Freshly ground white
  pepper

Briefly blanch each of the vegetables. Drain and refresh under cold running water. Cut the leaks, zucchini, and carrots lengthwise into 4 pieces.

Butter a terrine. Arrange some of the spinach leaves over the base and sides. Arrange the vegetables in layers, sprinkling some of the chervil between layers.

In a bowl, beat together the whole eggs, egg yolks, milk and pepper. Carefully pour this mixture over the layered vegetables. Place the remaining spinach leaves on top.

Cover the terrine with greaseproof paper; put on the lid. Stand the terrine on a wire rack in a baking dish half-filled with water. Bake in a preheated 150°C (300°F) oven for 1¼ hours.

Remove the lid and paper. Turn off the heat but leave the terrine in the oven for another 5 minutes. (The terrine should be delicately firm to the touch.) Remove from the oven; set aside to cool without chilling. (If made in advance and refrigerated, terrine should be allowed to come back to room temperature to serve.)

Cut into thick slices and serve with Champagne Vinegar Dressing (see recipe, *page 34*). Garnish with sprigs of fresh chervil.

Serves 6 to 8

Ham · Hocks · with
Coarse-grained · Mustard · Vinaigrette

I seldom seem to have enough leftover champagne to add to my cask of vinegar, so I have to buy my requirements! This recipe was given to me by a friend who begged it from a chef in the Champagne district of France.

1 tablespoon olive oil
1 carrot, finely chopped
1 celery stalk, with leaves,
  finely chopped
1 medium white onion,
  finely chopped
2 sprigs of thyme

2 bay leaves (fresh, if
  possible)
½ teaspoon peppercorns
2 whole cloves
6 smoked ham hocks
1 tablespoon white wine
  vinegar

Mustard Vinaigrette

1⅓ cups (10½ fl oz) virgin
olive oil
⅓ cup (2½ fl oz)
champagne vinegar

2 tablespoons coarse-
grained mustard
Freshly ground pepper

Heat the oil in a large saucepan. Stir in the chopped vegetables and herbs. Add the peppercorns and cloves and cook for about 3 minutes over moderate heat.

Add the hocks; cover with cold water. Bring to a boil. Reduce the heat to a simmer and cover the pan. Simmer gently for about 2½ hours.

Prepare the dressing: Combine all of the ingredients in a bowl and whisk vigorously until blended to a thick consistency.

To serve, remove the fat and skin from the hocks, cut the meat carefully from the bones, keeping it in as large portions as possible. Arrange the meat on serving plates, spoon on the dressing. Serve with a salad, featuring some bitter greens such as endive and radicchio.

Serves 6

Savoury · Fruit · Salad

Serve this fragrant salad with cold roast poultry or ham. It is particularly good with sliced turkey breast.

½ canteloupe (rockmelon)
½ green melon
(honeydew)
Champagne vinegar
dressing (see recipe, page
34)

750 g (1½ lb) watermelon
1 cup grapes
Ground ginger
Mint leaves for garnish

Peel the canteloupe and green melons, discarding the seeds. Cut the flesh into thin slices. Using a melon baller, scoop the watermelon flesh into small balls. Arrange the melon slices, balls and grapes on a serving platter; sprinkle with the ginger.

Make the dressing. Pour over the fruits. Chill for at least 1 hour. Garnish with mint leaves.

Serves 6

Champagne · Vinegar · Dressing

¾ cup (6 fl oz) grapeseed *Pinch of sugar*
oil or extra-light olive oil *Salt*
3 tablespoons champagne *Freshly ground white*
vinegar *pepper*

Combine all of the ingredients in a jar and shake (screw the lid on firmly) until well blended or whisk until well mixed.

Makes 1 cup (8 fl oz)

Malt Vinegar

Malt vinegar bears the same relationship to beer and ale as wine vinegar does to wine. It originated in the breweries of northern Europe as a way of disposing of soured beer. Malt vinegar was manufactured in England as early as the mid-1600s, under the name "alegar", with its obvious relationship to vinegar. It soon became known as vinegar.

The process of making malt vinegar is similar to beer manufacture. Malted barley is mashed, heated with water, and fermented into a crude type of beer known as "gyle". This beer is then dripped through plastic or steel vats filled with wood (usually beech) shavings. Acetobacters (vinegar bacteria) are introduced to assist the formation of acetic acid. The vinegar is then filtered and matured, and the resulting clear liquid is coloured with caramel.

Malt vinegar is particularly popular in England, where it is the traditional accompaniment to fish and chips and commonly used as an ingredient in old-fashioned mint sauce for roast lamb.

Robust in flavour and usually dark brown in colour, it is particularly suitable for recipes that use a variety of highly spiced ingredients, for example, pickles, chutneys and relishes. It contributes a hearty flavour and is also more economical than wine vinegars — a bonus in the kitchen!

Apple · and · Raisin · Chutney

Because of the robust flavours of other ingredients, malt vinegar is an excellent choice for this hearty chutney. Serve with cold meats and cheeses.

2 kg (4½ lb) cooking apples
750 g (1½ lb) seedless raisins
300 ml (10 fl oz) malt vinegar
300 ml (10 fl oz) white wine vinegar

500 g (1 lb) sugar
60 g (3 oz) salt (less, if preferred)
3 garlic cloves, finely chopped
60 g (2 oz) mustard seeds
30 g (1 oz) ground ginger
1 cinnamon stick

Peel and chop the apples, discarding the cores and seeds. Place in a heavy-based saucepan or preserving pan. (Do not use copper or aluminium.)

Add the raisins, vinegars, sugar, salt and garlic. Bring to a boil. Simmer for about 45 minutes.

Add the mustard seeds, ginger and cinnamon stick and simmer gently, stirring occasionally, for 10 minutes. Cover with a teatowel and allow to stand overnight.

Next day, bring to a boil. Simmer for 10 minutes, watching carefully to ensure it does not boil.

Spoon into warm sterile jars and seal.

Makes about four 250 g (8 oz) jars

Green · Tomato · Chutney

I like to use up the last tomatoes that linger on the bush, reluctant to ripen in the ever-shortening days of late summer, and I have found this recipe to be a good way of ensuring they do not go to waste.

1½ kg (3 lb) green tomatoes
1.2 l (40 fl oz) malt vinegar
500 g (1 lb) brown sugar

Salt (optional)
Freshly ground pepper
1 teaspoon mustard seed, or 1 teaspoon dry mustard

½ teaspoon ground   6 whole cloves
  cinnamon   2 star anise (if available)
1 teaspoon ground ginger   1 large onion, finely
1 teaspoon ground allspice   chopped

Cut the tomatoes into small pieces. Place in a non-reactive preserving pan or large saucepan. Add the vinegar, sugar, salt and pepper.

Cook over gentle heat until the sugar dissolves. Add the spices and onion. Simmer for 1½ to 2 hours, until thickened and well flavoured. Set aside to cool completely. Stir well and spoon into clean, dry jars. Seal tightly.

Makes about four 250 g (8 oz) jars

Dried · Apricot · Chutney

The great advantage of this spicy chutney is that it can be made at any time of the year — not just when we are able to harvest summer's bounty.

500 g (1 lb) dried apricots   Juice of 2 oranges
650 g (1¼ lb) white   Rind of 1 lemon
  onions, finely chopped   3½ cups malt vinegar
250 g (8 oz) raisins,   1 teaspoon dry mustard
  chopped   ½ teaspoon ground
2 whole cloves, finely   cinnamon
  chopped   ½ teaspoon ground allspice
Grated rind of 2 oranges

Soak the apricots in warm water overnight. Next day, drain and finely chop.

Combine all of the ingredients in a non-reactive preserving pan or large saucepan. Simmer over gentle heat, stirring from time to time to prevent burning, for about 1 hour or until thick and pulpy.

Pour into hot sterilised jars and seal with wax.

Makes about four 250 g (8 oz) jars

Farmhouse · Tomato · Sauce

A very useful way of taking advantage of the glut of tomatoes that often fills the markets (or home gardens) in late summer, you can enjoy the rich flavour of summer all winter long with this sauce. Use lusciously ripe tomatoes for best results.

3 kg (7 lb) tomatoes, sliced	*1¾ cups (14 fl oz) malt*
2 tablespoons salt	*vinegar*
2 cooking apples cored and	*1 teaspoon coarsely ground*
chopped	*pepper*
375 g (12 oz) onions,	*1 teaspoon ground cloves*
chopped	*½ teaspoon ground nutmeg*
180 g (6 oz) sugar	*½ teaspoon ground ginger*

Lay the sliced tomatoes on a platter. Sprinkle with the salt; set aside for about 1 hour.

Combine the apples and onions in a preserving pan or large heavy non-reactive saucepan. Add the sugar, vinegar and spices. Bring to a boil. Add the drained tomato slices. Simmer gently for 2 hours until pulpy in consistency and the flavours are well blended. Push through a coarse sieve or purée in a food processor.

Return to a clean saucepan and simmer for 45 to 60 minutes, or until the sauce is moderately thick. (Remember that the sauce must be of a consistency that can be poured from the bottle, rather than spooned from a jar like chutney.)

When the mixture is of the right consistency, allow to cool a little. Pour into sterilised bottles. (A funnel makes this task very much easier.) When sauce is quite cold, screw lids on firmly and store in a dark pantry or cupboard.

Makes about four 250 g (8 fl oz) bottles

Red · Plum · Sauce

When I was a child, self sown plum trees proliferated in our garden and in surrounding paddocks. A joy when the trees were lace-like with blossoms, it became a nightmare for Mum and Nanna when the time came to "use up" those omnipresent plums! Jams, chutneys, stewed plums all proliferated in our kitchen, but it is the pungent aroma of the plum sauce that I remember. Now that I have to buy or beg for plums, I treat them with more respect. But I still like to make up at least one batch of this sauce each year. It will certainly keep well until the following summer when once again your plum trees demand that you use their bounty.

2¼ kg (5 lb) red plums, stoned
2¾ kg (6 lb) onions, sliced
1.2 l (40 fl oz) malt vinegar
250 g (½ lb) sultanas
60 g (2 oz) dry mustard
30 g (1 oz) ground allspice
30 g (1 oz) green ginger, finely grated or chopped
15 g (½ oz) small hot chilies, or ½ teaspoon hot chili powder
15 g (½ oz) turmeric
½ teaspoon ground nutmeg
½ teaspoon ground cinnamon
6 whole cloves
500 g (1 lb) sugar

Place the plums and onions in a non-reactive large preserving pan or saucepan. Add half of the vinegar, the sultanas, mustard, allspice, ginger, chilies turmeric, nutmeg, cinnamon and cloves.

Bring to a boil. Simmer for 30 minutes. Push through a coarse sieve; return to a clean preserving pan. Add the remaining vinegar, and the sugar.

Simmer for 30 minutes, or until the mixture is of a good consistency for pouring. Set aside to cool completely. Bottle and seal firmly. Allow to mellow for at least 1 week before serving with cold meats, cheese, etc. It is particularly delicious spread on thickly buttered wholemeal bread topped with tasty cheese slices.

Makes about six 250g (8 oz) jars

Kate · Murphy's · Worcestershire · Sauce

This recipe was in a handwritten notebook picked up in an "op shop" many years ago. Other recipes in the book are dated 1934, so presumably this was of the same period.

2.25 l (9 cups) plus ½ cup (4 fl oz) malt vinegar
1 cup (10 oz) golden syrup
1 cup (10 oz) plum jam
125 g (4 oz) garlic, finely chopped

30 g (1 oz) whole cloves   1 tablespoon cayenne
1 tablespoon ground   pepper
  ginger

Combine all of the ingredients in a large non-reactive saucepan. Bring to a boil. Simmer for 2 hours; strain. Bottle when cold; set aside for at least 2 weeks before using.

Makes about five 250 g (8 oz) jars

Cider Vinegar

Cider vinegar has been around for as long as apple cider has been turning sour. Enthusiasts have claimed that it cures arthritis and the common cold, aids digestion, promotes fertility in cows, and assists in weight reduction. Some of the best apple ciders are still sold in health food stores.

Good apple cider vinegar starts with whole apples. The apples are ground into pulp, then cold-pressed to extract cider, which is poured into wooden casks where the natural sugars ferment into alcohol. The alcoholic cider is transferred to other wooden casks where it is exposed to air, which turns the alcohol to acetic acid. The cider vinegar is then aged until it develops a rich, full flavour.

Many of the cheap brands are made with apple cores and peelings, and then artificially infused with oxygen and bottled without ageing.

Cider vinegar is easy to make at home, but expect it to be cloudy — commercial types owe their crystal clarity to filtering. Start with a pure alcoholic apple cider that has no preservatives. Strain it through a clean tea-towel (to remove any sediment) into a crock or dark-coloured glass jar or bottle, leaving some space at the top. Cover the cider with muslin or cheesecloth and leave it in a dark cupboard for about four months. When the vinegar mother forms on top, taste the liquid to check the flavour. If the flavour is weak, leave the vinegar for another month, then check it again.

Instead of starting from scratch you can speed up the process by adding a vinegar mother to alcoholic apple cider. You can also create a substitute cider vinegar by mixing equal quantities of apple cider and white wine vinegar and leaving it for a few days.

Cider vinegar's most common use is for pickling, although it can also be used as a condiment: Sprinkle it into soups and stews and over fruit salads and steamed vegetables.

Experiment with this cider yourself. Use it as the base for dressings, savoury jellies and molds, and in pork dishes and savoury apple recipes. Another tip: It makes an excellent substitute for rice vinegar in Chinese and Japanese cooking.

Vegetarian · Wontons · with · Dipping Sauce

Use delectable little summer vegetables to create this flavoursome dish. Use your own favourite dipping sauce, if preferred.

1 tablespoon peanut oil
2 garlic cloves, finely
   chopped or crushed
1 teaspoon peeled and
   finely chopped fresh
   ginger
4 small zucchini
   (courgettes), coarsely
   grated
2 small carrots, coarsely
   grated
1 small ear of corn,
   stripped of kernels

2 spring onions (scallions),
   chopped
2 tablespoons finely
   chopped red capsicum
   (bell pepper)
3 tablespoons hoisin sauce
2 teaspoons dry sherry and
   ½ teaspoon finely grated
   fresh ginger
16 wonton wrappers
Peanut or soy oil for deep
   frying

Dipping Sauce

¾ cup (6 fl oz) pineapple   · 2 tablespoons brown sugar
   juice   1 tablespoon soy sauce
½ cup (4 fl oz) water   A few drops of chili sauce
3 tablespoons cider vinegar   1 tablespoon arrowroot

In a large skillet, heat the oil and sauté garlic and ginger until soft. Add the grated zucchini, carrot and corn kernels; cook gently until the liquid runs from the zucchini.

Remove the pan from the heat and add the spring onions and capsicum. Add the hoisin sauce and ginger wine; mix together.

Place 1 tablespoon of the mixture into the centre of each wonton skin. Moisten the edges and pinch tops firmly together to form little pouches.

Heat the oil to about 180°C (350°F). Deep fry the wontons in batches for a couple of minutes, until crisp and golden. Drain on kitchen paper and serve with the dipping sauce.

To make the sauce, combine all of the ingredients except the arrowroot and simmer in a non-reactive saucepan. Bring to a simmer. Blend together arrowroot and sufficient water to make a paste. Add to the pan and stir until the simmering sauce thickens and clears. Simmer and stir for another 2 minutes. Allow to cool slightly.

Makes about 16

Home-pickled · Cucumbers

A limp pickled cucumber is just not worth eating. These home-pickled ones have a terrific crunch as the sharp juices tickle the palate — delicious! If possible, use coarse pickling salt in this recipe. If you find it difficult to buy, your friendly local butcher can probably be coaxed to supply a cupful.

750 g to 1 kg (1½ to 2 lb)   1 garlic clove, slivered
  small cucumbers   1 whole clove
1 teaspoon black   Generous sprig of dill or
  peppercorns   aniseed
¾ teaspoon mustard seeds   ½ teaspoon dill seeds

1.2 l (40 fl oz) cider	*600 ml (20 fl oz) water*
vinegar	*60 g (2 oz) pickling salt*

Wash and pat dry the cucumbers. Pack neatly into a large jar.

Add the peppercorns, mustard seeds, garlic, clove, dill sprig and dill seeds.

Pour the vinegar into a large non-reactive saucepan. Add the water and salt and bring to a boil.

Allow to cool. Pour over the cucumbers, ensuring they are well covered. Seal with a plastic or china lid (to prevent corrosion) and allow to stand for 1 week before using.

Makes about four 250 g (8 oz) jars

NOTE: If preferred, white wine vinegar may be substituted for the cider vinegar.

Lemon · Chutney

This heavenly chutney is excellent with cold meats and served as an accompaniment to curries. It is particularly good with a chicken curry or a vegetable curry.

500 g (1 lb) onions	*500 g (1 lb) light brown or*
6 medium lemons	*white sugar*
Salt	*1 teaspoon dried allspice*
600 ml (20 fl oz) cider	*125 g (4 oz) seedless*
vinegar	*raisins*
60 g (2 oz) mustard seeds	

Peel and chop onions finely. Wash the lemons and cut into small pieces, removing all the pips. Place into a bowl and sprinkle with salt. Allow to stand overnight. Drain the next day.

Combine all of the ingredients in a heavy-based non-reactive saucepan. Bring to a boil (a dab of butter on top will help prevent the chutney from boiling over). Simmer for about 45 minutes or until thick and flavoursome.

Spoon into sterilised warm jars and seal. Allow to mellow for about 1 week before using.

Makes about four 250 g (8 oz) jars

Pickled · Pears

Delectable with most cold meats or curries, I like to have a good supply of these pickles, prepared when pears are plentiful and therefore cheap. They are also most palatable served with cheese and bread, or sliced into a salad.

1 kg small firm cooking pears
Whole cloves
1 small piece of green ginger, peeled and crushed
Small piece of cinnamon stick

Thinly peeled rind of half a small lemon
1 teaspoon allspice berries
500 g (1 lb) white sugar (more or less, to taste)
500 ml (16 fl oz) cider vinegar

Peel and core the pears, cut into quarters. Press a clove into each piece of pear and place the pears in a large jar.

Place ginger, cinnamon stick, lemon rind and allspice berries into a piece of muslin and tie into a small bag.

Dissolve the sugar in the vinegar, stirring often; tip into the jar and add the little pouch of spices.

Makes about four 250 g (8 oz) jars

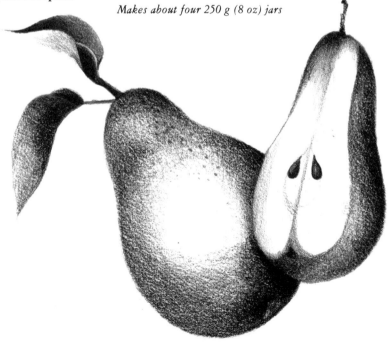

Cumberland · Sauce

This traditional sauce is excellent with corned beef; it may be bottled and stored in the refrigerator until required.

250 g (8 oz) redcurrant jelly	1 teaspoon prepared Dijon mustard
1 small onion, very finely chopped	2 tablespoons cider vinegar, or to taste
Rind of 2 oranges, cut into fine julienne	¼ cup (2 fl oz) port
Rind of 2 lemons, cut into fine julienne	Salt (optional)
	Freshly ground pepper

Gently melt the jelly in a heavy pan or in a microwave oven. Add the onion, rinds and mustard. Stir over low heat for 1 to 2 minutes. Stir in the vinegar. Add the port and salt and pepper to taste.

Simmer, stirring occasionally for about 20 minutes or until the sauce thickens. Spoon into small jars; cool. Seal tightly.

Makes 2½ to 3 cups (20 to 24 fl oz)

Spiced · Peaches

Use golden clingstone peaches for best results. Using these fruits, the pickle will mature and mellow in the jar for up to several years.

1 kg (2 lb) yellow peaches	6 whole cloves
500 g (1 lb) light brown sugar	Piece of cinnamon stick
300 ml (10 fl oz) cider vinegar or white wine vinegar	1 vanilla pod (bean)
	2 bay leaves (fresh, if possible)
	Kumquats

Blanch the peaches briefly and remove the skins. Halve the fruit and discard the stones.

Combine the sugar, vinegar, spices and bay leaves in a non-reactive preserving pan or large saucepan. Simmer gently until the sugar dissolves.

Add the peach halves, a few at a time, and the kumquats. Simmer for about 5 minutes, or until they begin to soften.

Place a kumquat in the bottom of each sterilised preserving jar (these are just to add a whisper of flavour). Add the peach halves, taking care not to cram them into the jars.

Strain the syrup, discarding the cloves.

Break the cinnamon stick and vanilla pod into pieces. Tear the bay leaves. Add these to each jar. Pour in the syrup.

Seal firmly, placing vinegar-proof covering under the lids. Allow to mature for at least one month.

Makes about four 250g (8 oz) jars

Baked · Beans · for · a · Barbecue

Use canned beans for a quick and easy version of this recipe, perfect for a family barbecue.

2 cans (440 g each; 1 lb each) baked beans
2 tablespoons oil
4 medium tomatoes, peeled and chopped
3 spring onions (scallions), chopped
1 garlic clove, very finely chopped
2 tablespoons cider vinegar
1 tablespoon treacle, golden syrup or corn syrup
1 tablespoon dark brown sugar
1 teaspoon sweet paprika, or ½ teaspoon hot paprika
1 teaspoon dry mustard
Freshly ground pepper

Remove the beans from the tins and set aside.

Heat the oil in a non-reactive skillet. Add the tomatoes, onions and garlic and cook gently until softened but not cooked. Stir in the vinegar, treacle, sugar, paprika, mustard and pepper. Cook for about 10 minutes.

Add the baked beans and mix gently. Cook for 5 to 8 minutes, or until the dish is well heated.

Serve with barbecued meats.

Serves 6 to 8

Sweet · and · Sour · Lentils

This is a splendid dish for those vegetarians who like something a little different.

2 tablespoons extra-light olive oil
1 small onion, finely chopped
½ garlic clove, finely chopped
2 tablespoons wholemeal (whole wheat) flour
1½ cups (12 fl oz) vegetable stock

2 tablespoons apple cider vinegar
2 tablespoons honey
1 teaspoon coarse-grained mustard
1 tablespoon soy sauce
2½ cups (12½ oz) cooked golden lentils (brown may be used, but do not look as appealing)

Heat the olive oil in a shallow saucepan and lightly sauté the onion and garlic. Stir in the flour a little at a time until well blended. Gradually add the stock, stirring constantly until the sauce thickens. Add the vinegar, honey, mustard and soy sauce and cook gently for 10 minutes.

Combine the sauce and the cooked lentils and mix lightly but thoroughly. Spoon into a buttered shallow casserole dish. Bake at 150°C (300 °F) for 30 minutes.

Serve with plenty of cooked vegetables of your choice.

Serves 4

Marinated · Cauliflower

Serve this as part of a spread of delicious appetisers or as a wonderful summer salad to serve with cold meats. Particularly good when served with smoked meats.

1 small white cauliflower
Juice of 1 large lemon
½ cup (4 fl oz) light olive oil
¼ cup (2 fl oz) cider vinegar

¼ cup (2 fl oz) water
1 tablespoon shredded orange zest
1 garlic clove, finely chopped
½ teaspoon fresh thyme, or ¼ teaspoon dried thyme

2 spring onions (scallions),
  very finely chopped
1 small red capsicum (bell
  pepper), cut into julienne
  or very finely chopped
Juice of 1 orange

Pepper
1 tablespoon finely
  chopped parsley
Rind of 1 orange, cut into
  julienne
Fresh herbs, for garnish

Cut the cauliflower into small florets, discard stems. Drop the florets into lightly salted boiling water and cook for 3 minutes. Drain, refresh under cold, running water and drain again. Place in a bowl; set aside.

Combine the oil, vinegar, water, orange zest, garlic and thyme in a non-reactive saucepan. Bring to a boil and remove from the heat. Stir in the onions, pepper julienne, orange juice and pepper.

Pour the marinade over the cauliflower and toss lightly. Set aside to cool. Cover and refrigerate overnight, tossing occasionally.

To serve, drain the cauliflower and arrange on a platter. Sprinkle with the parsley and garnish with fresh herbs and orange rind julienne.

Serves 8

Salad · of · Mixed · Beans

Several years ago I conducted a cookery school that included "Healthy Cooking" classes. This was a popular recipe with students. Make it in advance and allow the flavours to meld and mellow.

1 cup (6 oz) cooked or
  canned red kidney beans
½ cup (3 oz) cooked or
  canned white beans
½ cup (3 oz) cooked or
  canned chick peas
250 g (8 oz) green string
  beans, cut into 5 cm (2
  inch) lengths and
  steamed or boiled

250 g (8 oz) baby
  mushrooms, halved
2 tablespoons olive oil
½ red onion, thinly sliced
⅓ cup (2 oz) finely
  chopped parsley, or ⅓
  cup (2 oz) Italian (flatleaf) parsley leaves
1 garlic clove, finely
  chopped

Dressing

⅓ (2½ fl oz) cup cider
   vinegar
⅓ cup (2½ fl oz) olive oil
2 tablespoons honey
Salt (optional)

Freshly ground pepper
Salad greens, for serving
Italian (flatleaf) parsley,
   for garnish

Drain the canned or cooked beans, chick peas and string beans. Sauté the mushrooms in the olive oil for just 1 minute. Combine all ingredients except the dressing and toss together.

Whisk together all of the dressing ingredients. Pour over the salad and mix lightly but thoroughly. Allow to marinate for at least 1 hour before serving.

To serve, arrange the greens around the outer edge of a platter. Spoon the bean salad in the center. Garnish with Italian parsley leaves or sprigs.

Serves 6 to 8

Old-fashioned
Treacle · Toffee

Vinegar turns up as an ingredient in unexpected places. I can remember the sharply sweet smell of this toffee as Nanna cooked it — and the impatient small girl who could hardly wait until it was cold enough to eat!

500 g (1 lb) brown sugar
500 g (1 lb) treacle or corn
   syrup

3 tablespoons cider vinegar
125 g (4 oz) butter

Place the sugar, treacle and vinegar into a large non-reactive saucepan, and stir carefully over low heat until the sugar dissolves. (Try to avoid smearing the mixture up the sides of the saucepan — this can cause crystallising. Wash down the sides of the pan with a small brush dipped in water, if you want to be sure to avoid this problem.)

Bring the mixture very slowly to a boil. Boil for about 10 minutes, watching carefully to ensure it does not burn.

Gradually add the butter in thin slices, stirring as each small piece is added. Continue to boil until the toffee forms small balls when dropped into a bowl of cold water. (Keep changing the water after each test.)

Remove from the heat and allow the toffee to stand for 1 to 2 minutes. Pour gently into a 23 cm (9 inch) tin to a thickness of about 1 cm (½ inch).

When cool, but not firm, cut into squares with a blunt knife. Leave in the tin until cold.

When toffee is cold, break into squares. Wrap in waxed paper or foil or store in a tightly sealed container.

Makes about 20 squares

Apple · and · Thyme · Jelly

This is superb with cold meats and unexpectedly good with a cheddar cheese and home-made bread sandwich. Mmmm.

2 kg (5 lb) Granny Smith	*About 2½ cups (20 oz)*
cooking apples	*granulated sugar*
2 cups (16 fl oz) water	*Sprigs of fresh thyme,*
2 tablespoons thyme leaves	*washed and dried*
1 cup (8 fl oz) cider	
vinegar	

Rinse the apples. Roughly chop. Place the apples in a preserving pan with the water and thyme leaves. Bring to the boil. Simmer, uncovered, for 45 minutes or until soft and pulpy.

Stir in the vinegar. Boil for another 5 minutes.

Pour the mixture into a jelly bag or muslin and leave to drip over a pan or dish for 12 hours. (Do not squeeze the pulp in the muslin as this spoils the clarity of the jelly.) Measure the liquid. Add 1 cup (8 oz) sugar for each cup of liquid. Return the mixture to a clean pan and bring slowly to a boil. Stir constantly until the sugar dissolves. Boil vigorously, without stirring, for 10 to 15 minutes, or until a "set" is obtained (drop a teaspoon full onto a chilled saucer; it is set when it is slightly firm to touch).

Skim off any surface scum and stir mixture.

Pour the jelly into warm, dry jars. Cover with clean jam covers or warm paraffin. Label and store on a cool, dry shelf.

Makes about four 250g (8 oz) jars

Rice Vinegar

The Chinese were making vinegar from rice wine 3,000 years ago. It is an ingredient in many recipes, but its main used is as a condiment. It is delicious as a dip for seafood and for steamed dim sum, and it is also used to highlight the flavour of soups and stews. Rice vinegar can be red, black or white.

Chinese red vinegar is made from red rice. Used as a dip for fried foods, its clean taste seems to cut their richness. It is also an excellent addition to shark's fin soup and a traditional accompaniment to steamed crabs.

Chinese black vinegar has a rich, sweet flavour reminiscent of balsamic vinegar. Its uses are similar to Chinese red vinegar, but its flavour is more robust.

Chinese white vinegar is a pale gold vinegar used mainly in sweet and sour dishes.

The Japanese make a more delicate variety of rice vinegar. Called *su*, it is an important ingredient in Japanese cuisine. One of its most common uses is with sushi rice, but its mild tartness makes it an ideal addition to delicately flavoured chicken, seafood and vegetable dishes. There is a wide range of Japanese vinegars. They include Aji Pon which is flavoured with citrus juice and soy sauce and is wonderful as a marinade for grilled meat; Tosazu vinegar which is flavoured with fish stock, sugar and soy sauce and is used mainly as a condiment with seafood and vegetable dishes; and Ume-Su which is made from plums and used with vegetables and tofu.

Prawns · with · Asparagus · and Snow · Peas

This looks attractive and tastes great sharpened with a dash of rice vinegar.

2 tablespoons peanut oil
500 g (1 lb) green
  (uncooked) prawns,
  peeled
1 garlic clove, thinly sliced
5 cm (2 inch) piece green
  ginger cut into fine
  shreds
1 teaspoon arrowroot
⅔ cup (5 fl oz) light
  chicken stock

1 tablespoon rice vinegar
250g (8 oz) canned
  bamboo shoots, drained
250 g (8 oz) trimmed
  asparagus spears, cut into
  5 cm (2 inch) lengths
150 g (5 oz) snow peas,
  topped and tailed

Heat the oil in a wok or pan. Add the prawns, garlic and ginger; stir-fry only until prawns turn pink. Remove from the pan and set aside.

Blend the arrowroot into a little of the chicken stock, stir into remaining stock and add the rice vinegar.

Add the vegetables to the wok and stir-fry only until tender-crisp. Return the prawns to the wok.

Add the sauce and stir until thickened and clear. (Add a dash of soy sauce, if desired.)

Serve with plain boiled or steamed rice.

Serves 4

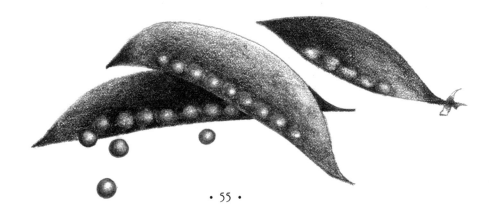

Marinated · Garfish

One of the sweetest of all fish, the bones often deter one from eating garfish. Ask your fishmonger to fillet four, so that you have eight fillets for this dish.

1 to 2 tablespoons sea salt
8 garfish (soft, white
* fleshed fish) fillets*
1 sheet kelp (seaweed such
* as Novior Kelp, available*
* in Asian grocery stores)*

1 cup (8 fl oz) rice vinegar
¼ cup (2 oz) sugar

Sprinkle the salt over the skin side of the fillets and allow to stand for 10 to 15 minutes.

Cut the sheet of kelp into 8 strips and place a piece under each fillet.

Mix together the vinegar and sugar, stirring until the sugar dissolves.

Place the fillets, with the kelp underneath, in a shallow dish. Pour on the marinade and allow to stand for 30 minutes.

Carefully lift out each fillet and place on an attractive serving plate. Serve with Horseradish Cream (see recipe, *page 13*) and soy sauce.

Serves 4

NOTE: The vinegar has the effect of breaking down the flesh of the fish and the texture is that of lightly cooked fish.

Steamed · Garlic · Chicken
with · Cucumber

This is a delicately flavoured Oriental-style dish in which the sauce plays an important role in its presentation. If rice vinegar is unavailable, substitute cider vinegar.

2 spring onions (scallions),
* roots and skin removed*
2.5 cm (1 inch) cube green
* ginger*
4 garlic cloves (less, if
* preferred)*

4 skinless chicken fillets
Salt (optional)
1 tablespoon rice wine or
* dry sherry*

2 small Lebanese (very
small) cucumbers

Fresh coriander leaves (if
available)

Sauce

3 tablespoons light soy
sauce
2 tablespoons rice vinegar
½ teaspoon Oriental
sesame oil
1 garlic clove, very finely
chopped

1 spring onion (scallion),
very finely chopped
1½ teaspoons slivered
green ginger

Crush the spring onion and the ginger with a cleaver or wooden mallet; cut each garlic clove into 2 or 3 slices.

Sprinkle salt on the chicken fillets. Place them on a plate in the base of a Chinese bamboo steamer basket. Place the spring onion, ginger and garlic on the fillets. Sprinkle on the rice wine.

Cover the bamboo steamer; place steamer over a saucepan of simmering water. Cook for about 20 minutes, or until the chicken fillets are tender and just cooked. Remove from the steamer and allow to cool. Cut into thin diagonal slices.

Cut the cucumbers lengthwise into wafer thin slices. Pile in the center of a plate. Arrange the chicken slices around it. Combine all of the sauce ingredients; whisk well. Pour over the chicken and cucumbers. Garnish with fresh coriander leaves, if available.

Serves 4

Beef · Sashimi

Despite the very high cost of beef in Japan, this is a popular dish. Japanese diners prefer the tender, fat-marbled beef from grain-fed cattle and of course the robust vinegar marinade provides plenty of flavour.

375 g (12 oz) eye filet of
beef
2 cups (16 fl oz) rice wine
vinegar
½ cup (4 oz) sugar

2 French shallots
(scallions), finely
chopped
2 cm (¾ inch) piece green
ginger, grated

Thinly slice the beef; cut into small squares.

Combine the vinegar, sugar, shallots and ginger in a bowl. Add the meat and marinate for up to 10 minutes.

Remove the beef from the marinade. Drain lightly. Serve on a platter, accompanied by shredded cucumber.

Serves 2 to 3

Plum · Glazed · Lamb · Cutlets

Oriental in flavour, little lamb cutlets are delicious served this way.

½ cup (5 oz) Chinese plum sauce
2 garlic cloves, finely chopped
2 tablespoons finely grated or chopped green ginger

2 tablespoons light soy sauce
2 tablespons rice vinegar
¼ teaspoon Chinese 5-spice mixture
12 lamb cutlets, well trimmed

Combine the plum sauce, garlic, ginger, soy sauce, vinegar and Chinese 5-spices in a small non-reactive saucepan. Simmer for 5 minutes.

Lightly brown the cutlets on each side under a preheated grill (broiler). Brush lavishly with the plum glaze on one side. Grill until brown and glossy, turn and brush glaze onto second side. Grill until cooked to taste.

Serve with steamed rice and lightly stir-fried vegetables such as a mixture of julienned carrots, snow peas, spring onions, etc.

Serves 4 to 6

Asian · Vegetarian · Salad

Arrange this on a black platter or lacquer tray for maximum visual appeal! Based on a Malaysian cuisine, the flavours are different but delectable.

500 g (1 lb) broccoli, broken into small florets

250 g (8 oz) green beans

125 g (4 oz) oyster
mushrooms
180 g (6 oz) bean sprouts

1 green capsicum (bell
pepper), seeded and cut
lengthwise into fine
strips
½ cucumber, seeded and
cut lengthwise into strips

Sauce

Juice of 2 lemons or limes
2 tablespoons peanut oil
2 tablespoons rice vinegar
¼ cup (2 oz) tahini
(sesame seed paste)

⅓ teaspoon finely crushed
dried red chili
2 garlic cloves, slivered

Marinade

60 g (2 oz) desiccated
coconut
½ cup (4 fl oz) hot water

1 tablespoon Oriental
sesame oil

Garnish

250 g (8 oz) tofu (bean
curd), cubed and deep
fried

Toasted sesame seeds
Coriander sprigs
(optional)

Prepare the vegetables, set aside. Lightly cook the broccoli and beans; allow to cool.

To make the sauce, combine all of the ingredients and set aside to allow the flavours to mature.

To make the marinade: Soak the coconut in the water for at least 1 hour. Spoon into muslin placed in a colander; strain off liquid. Squeeze to ensure all of the juice is extracted. Stir in sesame oil. Pour over the vegetables and marinate for 2 to 3 hours. Drain off vegetables and retain liquid.

Arrange piles of the different vegetables on a serving platter. Garnish with tofu and sesame seeds. Place the sauce, coconut and marinade in a food processor and blend until a thick sauce is created. Pass separately.

Salad may be garnished with coriander sprigs, if available.

Serves 4 to 6

Japanese · Pickled · Cabbage

The Japanese cuisine is rich in pickles, many of which are preserved in salt — rather difficult for Western palates to accept. This pickle is delicious and happily accompanies most Western dishes that would be acceptable with sauerkraut. I like it with hearty sausages such as bratwurst.

¼ head of tight-leafed
   cabbage
5 cups (40 fl oz) rice
   vinegar
2 tablespoons coarse salt

5 tablespoons sugar
2 cups (16 fl oz) water
Strips of rind from ½
   lemon

Core the cabbage; cut the cabbage into small chunks. Rinse and dry. Pack the pieces loosely into a preserving jar.

In a non-reactive saucepan, combine the vinegar, salt, sugar and water. Bring to a rapid boil. Pour the vinegar into the jar over the cabbage. Using a skewer, place pieces of lemon peel into the jars. Seal firmly with a non-metal lid. Do not use for several days.

The cabbage is served shredded in small bowls. A dash of soy may be added, if desired. This pickle keeps well, under refrigeration, for at least 6 weeks.

Serves 4

Japanese · Vinegared · Rice

¼ cup (2 fl oz) rice vinegar
1 tablespoon sugar
2 cups (8 oz) freshly
   cooked rice, cooled but
   not cold

2 tablespoons crumbled
   dried nori *(seaweed)*

Combine the vinegar and sugar in a bowl; stir until the sugar dissolves. Add the rice and seaweed and blend thoroughly.

To serve, tightly pack the mixture into an ice cream scoop or a small mold and unmold onto lettuce leaves. An alternative serving suggestion is to use sheets of *nori* as a wrapping. Spread it flat on the counter and spoon a thin layer of the rice onto it.

Arrange a row of pretty, salmon-pink pickled ginger down the center and firmly roll up the *nori* — rather like a jam filled Swiss roll! Press gently but firmly to seal. Wrap in plastic film and chill for a short time for ease of handling, then cut the roll into bite-size lengths.

These little rolls may be served with drinks or as part of a sushi platter.

Serves 4 to 6

Coconut Vinegar

It is not surprising that the coconut should yield a vinegar: People use every part of the coconut palm to make life more pleasant in countries where it grows freely. They use fronds for thatching roofs and making mats and baskets, the fibrous covering of the coconut for matting, ropes and brushes, and the dried flesh for copra, which yields the base for an oil used in soaps, candles, cosmetics and suntan oil. The coconut also provides a drink, and from the flesh comes shredded, flaked and desiccated coconut, plus the coconut milk and coconut cream used in Asian cooking.

But have you tried coconut vinegar? It has a somewhat musty flavour and a distinctive aftertaste. It's colourless and has a low acetic acid level, usually of about four percent.

Coconut vinegar is made from coconut that is mashed, heated with water and then fermented. The alcoholic liquid is then poured into large vats filled with wood shavings and left for several weeks until the alcohol turns to acetic acid.

Manufactured mainly in the Philippines, I like to use it in recipes with an Asian, particularly a Thai, influence.

Spiced · Chicken · Wings

Really tasty finger food, these spicy morsels may be served on a buffet table or as a substantial cocktail nibble.

1 kg (2 lb) chicken wings,
* tip trimmed off*
2 small red chilies, finely
* shredded and seeds*
* discarded*
5 tablespoons tomato
* purée*
5 tablespoons light olive
* oil or peanut oil*

2 tablespoons soy sauce
2 tablespoons coconut
* vinegar or white wine*
* vinegar*
1 tablespoon finely
* chopped green ginger*
3 garlic cloves, finely
* chopped*
Fresh coriander leaves

Scrape the flesh from the upper wing back towards the thick end, using a small, not too sharp knife. (This bone serves as a handle.)

Make the marinade by mixing all of the remaining ingredients, except the coriander leaves, in a bowl. Place the chicken wings into the marinade, turn to ensure they are evenly covered with the mixture. Cover and chill for at least 8 hours, preferably overnight.

Heat the oven to 220° C (450° F). Spread the chicken wings evenly over a lightly greased roasting dish; brush on the marinade. Cook for 20 to 25 minutes, turning once or twice during cooking.

Arrange on a platter; garnish with fresh coriander leaves.

Serves 4 to 6

NOTE: Parsley, basil or mint leaves may be used to garnish the chicken wings.

Sharp · Chicken · Satay

Serve these tasty satays at a barbecue in the backyard or at your dining table, cooked under a griller (broiler). I like to cook them on a little hibachi set out on my terrace. (I need to keep my giant poodle, Rosie, at bay — she believes *she* is a guest whenever I entertain outdoors!)

4 skinless chicken breasts　　*bamboo satay sticks*
　　　　　　　　　　　　　　　(soaked in cold water)

Marinade

½ cup (4 fl oz) coconut　　*2 garlic cloves, finely*
　milk　　　　　　　　　　*chopped*
1 tablespoon coconut　　　*1 teaspoon curry paste*
　vinegar　　　　　　　　　*½ teaspoon turmeric*
1 tablespoon brown sugar　*1 stalk of lemon grass,*
　or palm sugar　　　　　　*finely chopped (discard*
¼ cup (2 fl oz) soy sauce　　*coarse, woody section)*

Slice each chicken breast lengthwise into 5 or 6 pieces. Place in a shallow bowl.

Make the marinade: Blend the coconut milk, coconut vinegar and sugar in a food processor. Gradually add the soy sauce, garlic, curry paste, turmeric and lemon grass. Blend to a smooth paste.

Mix the marinade with the chicken strips. Stir gently and allow to marinate for 2 hours. Thread on to the soaked bamboo skewers. Cook on a barbecue or under a griller (broiler). Serve with Peanut Satay Sauce (see recipe, *below*).

Peanut Satay Sauce

2 cups (8 oz) roasted　　　*¼ cup (2 fl oz) tamarind*
　skinned peanuts　　　　　*water (2 teaspoons tama-*
6 garlic cloves, finely　　　*rind paste soaked in 6*
　chopped　　　　　　　　　*tablespoons water and*
6 small red chilies (yes, it　*strained)*
　is a hot sauce!), seeded　*1¾ cups (14 fl oz) coconut*
　and finely shredded　　　*milk*
90 g (3 oz) brown or palm　*2 tablespoons peanut oil*
　sugar

Crush the peanuts. Sauté the garlic in the oil. Add the peanuts, chilies and sugar. Mix well. Stir in the tamarind water and coconut milk. Continue stirring until well blended and hot. Cool and serve with the satays. Keeps well.

Mint · Marinated · Beef · Salad

Based on a Thai recipe, I have found coconut vinegar to be a compatible ingredient in this dish. I have also substituted basil leaves for mint or used ⅔ basil, ⅓ mint and the effect is pleasant and different.

1 kg (2 lb) lean filet or
sirloin steak, trimmed
⅓ cup (1 oz) coriander
leaves, finely chopped
1 garlic clove, finely
chopped
2 tablespoons soy sauce
2 tablespoons coconut
vinegar
1 tablespoon nam pla *(fish*
sauce)

30 g (1 oz) brown sugar
⅓ cup (1 oz) fresh mint
leaves
2 shallots (scallions), finely
sliced from tip to root
1 small red chili, seeded
and shredded
1½ cups (24 whole) cherry
tomatoes

Roast the beef for 45 to 50 minutes until medium rare (or preferred degree) in a baking dish. Set aside to cool.

Place the coriander leaves, garlic, soy sauce, coconut vinegar, *nam pla* and sugar in a food processor or blender; mix to a smooth paste.

Slice the beef as thinly as possible. Place the meat into a shallow dish with the marinade paste. Bruise half of the mint leaves, and add to the marinade. Allow to stand for at least 1 hour, turning the meat occasionally to ensure the marinade flavours it evenly.

Arrange the beef slices on a serving platter. Garnish with the shallots, chili, cherry tomatoes and remaining mint leaves.

Serves 6 to 8

Asian · Cucumber · Salad

This is particularly delicious served with fish dishes. I like to use the long, fleshy Continental cucumbers or the small Lebanese cucumbers; if I use the latter, I leave the skin and seeds intact and slice the cucumber thinly at an acute diagonal angle.

2 medium cucumbers, or
8 Lebanese cucumbers
1 tablespoon sugar
2 tablespoons coconut
vinegar
2 small red chilis, seeded
and very finely shredded

60 g (2 oz) roasted
unsalted peanuts,
chopped or finely crushed
2 shallots (scallions),
thinly sliced
Fresh coriander leaves
2 teaspoons nam pla *(fish*
sauce)

Halve cucumbers lengthwise; remove the seeds with a spoon. Slice thickly; place into a shallow dish.

Stir the sugar into the coconut vinegar. Add the cucumber and toss well until coated. Sprinkle on the chilies, peanuts, shallots and coriander leaves. Allow to marinate for about 1 hour.

Sprinkle on the *nam pla* just before serving.

Serves 6 to 8

Herb Vinegars

It is easy to make herb vinegars at home, and the beauty is that you can experiment and create your own combinations. I prefer to use home-made vinegar as the base, but don't be deterred from using commercial vinegar. Make sure, however, that it is of good quality, and delicate in flavour so as to allow the taste and fragrance of the herbs to be fully appreciated.

To create herb vinegars you will need: a good white or red wine vinegar, apple cider vinegar, or rice wine vinegar; an attractive bottle (it can be a wine or champagne bottle); cork or stopper (not metal); wooden skewers for poking herb flowers and leaves into place; and, of course, herbs (the proportion is up to you but as a general guide, about four tablespoons to 450 ml or 15 fl oz of vinegar).

There are two ways to make herb vinegars. The first is more time consuming and often preferred by experts, but the second is quick and easy, and quite satisfactory.

1. Bring vinegar to a boil and add the herbs, either fresh or dried; simmer for about half an hour, then cool. Strain and bottle the vinegar. Add a few sprigs of fresh herb for garnish and identification, before sealing the bottle.

2. Wash and dry the fresh herbs and tuck them into the bottle. Heat the vinegar without boiling, and pour it into the bottle. You can simply pour room temperature vinegar over the herbs (but warming it helps bring out

the flavour). Use wooden skewers to arrange the herbs attractively. Allow it to cool before sealing. Stand the sealed bottles in sunlight. A windowsill is ideal. Taste after two weeks. When the flavour is satisfactory you can strain off the herbs or leave them in the bottle — it's a matter of appearance.

It is important to avoid using metal stoppers: The acidity of vinegar will corrode metal and it may spoil the flavour of the vinegar. Use corks, or ceramic or glass stoppers. If you are bottling vinegar for sale or for gift-giving, spend time on presentation. I like to cut out heavy coffee-coloured parchment tags, thread them with hand-spun yarn, coarse string or fine satin ribbon, and tie them around the neck of the bottle. Handwritten tags or labels will enhance the appearance, and, rather than bluntly specifying the type of vinegar on the label, use a little imagination. Your basil vinegar, for instance, could be "the essense of summer captured in a fragrant and delicately flavoured fine wine vinegar"!

Most herbs are suitable, although parsley does not contribute a lot of flavour — nor does borage — but I like to use the pretty blue flowers as decoration. Basil, thyme, rosemary, bay leaves, dill, chervil and lemon balm are all particularly suitable and will generously endow the vinegar with their distinctive flavour and perfume. Pick the leaves early in the day, and wash and dry them before use. You need fewer of the robust herbs, but use a delicate herb such as salad burnet in quantity for the flavour to develop well. For extra flavour, you may add a few peppercorns, a clove of garlic, a few shreds of chili or a twist of lemon or orange peel. Be sure to choose compatible flavours: for instance, rosemary and orange peel, or basil and garlic.

To retain the full flavour of the herb vinegar, once the flavours have developed and matured, store it in a cool, dark cupboard.

Herb vinegars are wonderful additions to the larder. Use them in dressings, pickles, soups and casseroles, and for deglazing pans. It's a lovely way to preserve the flavour of summer herbs for use in winter.

Thyme · Vinegar

I always like to have some of this on hand — great to deglaze a pan for a steak. Simply pour a little into the pan in which a filet steak has been cooked, add a little tomato purée, a dash of Worcestershire sauce and a grind of pepper. Spoon it onto the steak and you have a gourmet dish.

About 10 generous sprigs of thyme (with a few flowerheads, if available)	*500 ml (16 fl oz) white wine or cider vinegar*

Crush the sprigs of thyme with the fingertips so the leaves release their volatile oils. Place the sprigs into a bottle. Pour on cold or warmed vinegar. Seal and set aside in a warm place for up to 2 weeks before using.

Makes 500 ml (16 fl oz)

Rosemary · Vinegar

This is a beautiful vinegar, with a wonderful fragrance that greets you when the bottle is uncorked. I like to make it with white wine vinegar, but add just a dash of red wine (not vinegar) to create a delicate blush of colour.

Rub the leaves firmly with the fingertips before placing them into the bottle; this helps release the volatile oils and enhances the flavour.

About 10 sprigs of rosemary (with a few flowerheads, if available) 2 teaspoons honey	*500 ml (16 fl oz) white wine vinegar 1 to 2 tablespoons dry red wine*

Crush the leaves gently; tuck the sprigs into the bottle. Stir together the honey, vinegar, and red wine; mix well. Pour into the bottle; shake.

Stopper firmly and stand on a sunny ledge or outside in a spot that captures the sunshine for a couple of weeks.

Use in dressings, to deglaze pans, or add a splash to fruit salads and stewed fruits.

Makes about 500 ml (16 fl oz)

Chive · Vinegar

The delicate onion flavour of chives makes this an ideal vinegar to sprinkle on salads. For a really pretty effect, arrange a few chive flowers and buds among the wispy chive stems.

*A small handful of chive
greens, of varying
lengths
A few chive flowers and
buds, still on their stalks*

*Several pink peppercorns
500 ml (16 fl oz) white
wine vinegar*

Arrange the chive greens and flowers in a bottle; add the peppercorns. Gently pour in the wine and re-arrange the herbs, if necessary, with a satay stick. Do not use for 2 weeks.

Makes about 500 ml (16 fl oz)

Dill · or · Fennel · Vinegar

Use this strongly flavoured herb vinegar with fish or cabbage dishes. It's good, too, with potato dishes. If you don't have access to a quanity of dill, don't overlook the wild fennel that often grows in paddocks. Pick the tender young growth, rinse it and use it as a substitute for the dill.

1 handful of dill sprigs, washed and dried	*500 ml (16 fl oz) white wine vinegar A few peppercorns*

Place the dill sprigs in a bottle of appropriate size. Pour on the vinegar, add the peppercorns and shake the bottle.

Stopper the bottle. Stand in a warm place until the flavour develops and matures.

Makes about 500 ml (16 fl oz)

Tarragon · Vinegar

Used as the base for béarnaise sauce when fresh tarragon is not available, tarragon vinegar may be made with newly picked French tarragon or the dried variety. (Do not use Russian tarragon. It is coarse, poorly flavoured and no substitute for the "real thing".)

¼ cup (one handful) fresh French tarragon leaves, lightly crushed, or 1 generous tablespoon dried tarragon	*600 ml (20 fl oz) white wine vinegar A few peppercorns (optional)*

Place the fresh or dried tarragon into a bottle. Pour on the vinegar; add the peppercorns if using. Stopper and allow to stand for at least 2 weeks before using. Vinegar may be strained or not, as preferred.

Makes about 600 ml (20 fl oz)

Basil · Vinegar

During its all-too-brief appearance in the summertime, I greedily use basil in as many dishes as possible. With squirrel-like enthusiasm I take precautions against those barren winter months when my beloved basil is not available and accordingly make quantities of pesto, freeze basil purée, make basil oils and of course basil vinegars! Although the beautifully fragrant sweet basil is the one we see most often and use most commonly, there is a wide variety of basils available, including the very beautiful purple-leafed variety, sometimes called opal basil.

I make up good quantities of the green basil vinegar, but it is the opal that I love... oh the joy of seeing those beautiful violet-ruby bottles offering promises of winter flavour and fragrance!

600 ml (20 fl oz) white wine vinegar

¾ cup (2 oz) basil leaves stripped from the stems (use, green or purple basil)

Combine the vinegar and slightly crushed basil leaves in a jar. Cover and seal. Let stand in a sunny spot over 2 or 3 weeks. If opal basil is used, the colour will change to a jewel-like translucence over this time.

Strain through muslin. Pour the vinegar into bottles and add a sprig of the appropriate basil.

Makes about 600 ml (20 fl oz)

Mint · Vinegar

The flavour of this will vary depending on the variety of mint used. For example, an eau-de-cologne mint will produce a perfumed, aromatic vinegar, whereas the more common lamb mint, winter mint or peppermint will create a vinegar which is versatile enough to be used as the basis for mint sauce or in any dish complemented by a minty flavour.

600 ml (20 fl oz) cider vinegar
1 teaspooon white sugar

1½ tablespoons mint leaves, lightly crushed

Place the leaves in a jar, add the sugar and stir well; add the mint leaves. Seal well and do not open for 2 or 3 weeks.

Makes 600 ml (20 fl oz)

Lemon · Balm · Vinegar

This prolific-grower, a close relative of the mint family, makes an excellent vinegar. Follow the instructions for Mint Vinegar (see recipe, *above*). If an even more pronounced citrus flavour is preferred, add some finely shredded lemon rind with the lemon balm leaves. I like to use this vinegar in a sweet-sour sauce or with chicken dishes.

Vinegar · with · a · Herbal · Quartet

It is worthwhile making a large quantity of this versatile herb vinegar. The combination of flavours offers a wide range of choices for its use in salad dressings, sauces, pan deglazing or as the vinegar base for special pickles. Just a few drops added to a commercial sauce or chutney gives it your personal stamp! This is an excellent vinegar for gift-giving. For an even more attractive appearance, strain off the herbs (which will lose their fresh green colour after a time) and replace them with a sprig of each of the herbs used just before you present your gift.

500 ml (16 fl oz) white	*borage leaves, basil*
wine vinegar	*leaves, mint leaves and*
One handful each of young	*chives*

Pick the herbs before the sun is on them. If necessary, wash and dry them carefully. Crush the leaves and pack them into a jar.

Bring the vinegar to a boil. Allow to cool a little and pour over the herbs. Cover the bottle tightly with a non-metal lid and leave it for 2 weeks, shaking the jar each day or turning it upside down on alternate days.

After about 2 weeks, strain the vinegar, pour into bottles and cork or stopper tightly.

Makes about 500 ml (16 fl oz)

A · Vinegar · of · Herbs · and · Spices

I love this vinegar and often present it as a gift in little "gourmet delight" baskets. It looks really pretty tucked into a tiny basket lined with a Laura Ashley style print, with a tiny posy of herbs and cottage flowers tied to the handle.

*2 tablespoons fresh
  marjoram or oregano leaves*
1 tablespoon mint leaves
*1 tablespoon French
  tarragon leaves (the
  Russian tarragon is
  unsuitable)*
*1 to 2 tablespoons fresh
  basil leaves*

*4 bay leaves (preferably
  fresh)*
1 l (32 fl oz) cider vinegar
5 whole cloves
½ teaspoon mustard seeds
½ teaspoon dill seeds
*½ teaspoon whole black
  peppercorns*
⅓ teaspoon allspice berries

Lightly crush all of the herb leaves; place them into a large glass jar. (A preserving jar is excellent.) Pour the vinegar into an enamelled or ceramic saucepan. Add all of the spices and bring to a boil. Simmer for about 5 minutes.

    Allow to cool a little. Pour the vinegar and spices over the herb leaves in the jar.

    When the vinegar is cold, seal the jar firmly and allow to stand for at least 2 weeks.

    Vinegar may then be strained and rebottled into smaller jars or bottles.

Makes about 4 cups (32 fl oz)

Asparagus · Spears · with · Hollandaise · Sauce

Perhaps the most elegant and delicious of all first courses, serve this simple dish when the first asparagus of spring is at its tender best.

1 kg (2 lb) asparagus spears

Hollandaise Sauce

3 tablespoons fennel flavoured vinegar (see recipe, page 71)	*90 to 125 g (3 to 4 oz) unsalted butter, softened*
5 peppercorns	*Salt (optional)*
1 small bay leaf (preferably fresh)	*Freshly ground pepper*
2 egg yolks	*A few sprigs of fresh chervil, if available*

Bring plenty of very lightly salted water to a boil in a large saucepan or an asparagus steamer. Plunge in the asparagus. (Break the stems where they "give" to ensure the woody parts have been removed). Cook for a maximum of 7 minutes and then drain and serve at once.

Whilst the asparagus cooks, make the hollandaise sauce: Boil the vinegar with the peppercorns, and bay leaf until reduced to 2 tablespoons. Pour into a bowl.

Using a wooden spoon, beat in the egg yolks and about 2 teaspoons of the butter.

Place the bowl over a saucepan of gently simmering water. Gradually add the butter in small pieces, whisking all the time. Be very careful that the sauce does not become too hot, otherwise it could separate. If that should happen, place the bowl into cold water. It is a good idea to have a large basin of chilled water standing by.

Remove from the heat immediately when all of the butter has been whisked in. Add salt and pepper to taste. Asparagus may be arranged on a serving platter with the sauce spooned over or served on individual plates and the sauce passed separately.

Serves 6

Avocado · and · Cucumber · Scoops

Smooth yet tangy, the cucumber flavour is sharpened and enhanced by the addition of herb vinegar.

2 small ripe avocadoes
2 medium cucumbers,
  peeled seeded and grated
2 cups (16 fl oz) reduced
  (low fat) cream
2 to 3 tablespoons sugar
  (or to taste)
3 tablespoons herb vinegar
  (see recipe, page 73)

1 tablespoon finely
  chopped parsley
Grated zest of 1 lemon or
  lime
Salt
White pepper to taste
Salad burnet sprigs for
  garnish, if available

Halve the avocadoes, discard the stones. Combine all of the ingredients, except the herb sprigs, and pour into the bowl of an ice cream machine. Process according to maker's instructions.

If not using a machine, combine the ingredients as above, but lightly whip the cream. Spoon into ice cream trays and allow to freeze until beginning to firm around the edges.

Spoon into a bowl, beat until smooth and pour back into ice cream trays. Freeze until firm, but not solid.

To serve, scoop into goblets and garnish with cucumber slices and salad burnet sprigs.

Serves 6 as an appetiser

Chilled · Lemon · Chicken

This is a beautiful summer dish, which may be cooked in advance for a luncheon. Low in kilojoules (calories), it is a perfect choice for the would-be slimmer!

1 roasting chicken, cut up
2 cups (16 fl oz) rich
  chicken stock
½ cup (4 fl oz) dry white
  wine
¼ cup (4 fl oz) tarragon
  vinegar (see recipe, page
  71)
1 thyme sprig
1 French tarragon sprig
1 large parsley sprig

1 bay leaf
6 whole peppercorns
1 garlic clove, halved
1 onion, thickly sliced
1 carrot, thickly sliced
½ lemon, sliced
Juice of ½ lemon
1 tablespoon grated lemon zest
Fresh lemon slices
Fresh French tarragon
  leaves

Remove skin and fat from the chicken portions; discard.

Combine the chicken stock, wine, vinegar, herbs, peppercorns, garlic, onion, carrot and sliced lemon in a large, shallow non-reactive saucepan. Add the chicken pieces. Simmer very gently for about 1 hour, or until the chicken pieces are very tender. Allow them to cool in the liquid.

Remove the chicken and arrange on an attractive serving platter. Skim every skerrick (isn't that a wonderful old word — I find it often in my grandmother's handwritten recipe books) of fat from the stock. Strain the cooking liquid through muslin. Add the lemon juice and the grated zest. Return to a saucepan and boil rapidly until the liquid is reduced to 1¼ to 2 cups. Adjust the seasonings to taste. Set aside to cool.

Pour the cooled liquid over the chicken pieces. Garnish with lemon slices and fresh tarragon leaves. Chill until the liquid has set to a deliciously tangy jelly.

Serves 5 to 6

Braised · Steak · and · Onions

An old-fashioned dish, savoury and satisfying for a winter meal. I remember it simmering away on the woodstove top when I was a little girl, but nowadays I cook it in the oven — either way gives excellent results.

1 kg (2 lb) skirt steak (or similar cut)	*3 tablespoons herb vinegar (see recipe, page 73)*
3 tablespoons oil	*1 bay leaf*
1 large onion, finely chopped	*1 small cinnamon stick*
2 garlic cloves, crushed or very finely chopped	*3 whole cloves*
	1 teaspoon sugar
1 cup (8 fl oz) tomato purée	*Salt (optional)*
	Freshly ground pepper
½ cup (4 fl oz) dry red wine	*750 g (1½ lb) small pickling onions*

Cut the beef into 5 cm (2 inch) cubes. Heat the oil in a skillet. Add the meat and brown on all sides. (You will need to do this in several batches.) Place the meat into a casserole dish.

Add the onion and garlic to the pan, adding a little more oil if necessary, and cook gently until softened.

Pour the tomato purée, wine and vinegar into the pan and simmer, stirring constantly and scraping the bottom of the pan. (We want to capture all that flavour!) Pour over the meat in the casserole.

Add the bay leaf, spices, sugar, salt and pepper. Cover and cook in a moderately low 160°C (375°F) oven for 1½ hours.

While the meat cooks, peel the onions and place in a bowl. Cover with boiling water and leave for 10 minutes. Drain well.

After the meat has cooked for the first 1½ hours, add the onions. Continue to cook for another 1 to 1¼ hours, or until the meat is tender. This dish freezes well.

If cooking on the stovetop, use a heavy-based saucepan and follow similar timing as for oven cooking. It also cooks well in a crockpot.

Serves 6

Trout · Piquant

Rosemary vinegar adds a delightful pungency to this dish. Serve with bland flavoured vegetables such as boiled potatoes and green beans. A lightly seasoned sliced tomato and onion salad is also a compatible accompaniment.

4 to 6 small trout	*¼ cup (2 fl oz) rosemary*
Seasoned flour, for coating	*vinegar (see recipe, page 69)*
Light olive oil or peanut	*⅓ cup (2½ fl oz) dry white wine*
oil, for frying	*Fresh rosemary sprigs, for*
3 garlic cloves, finely chopped	*garnish*

Wipe the fish and pat dry. Dip into the seasoned flour and coat lightly. Shake gently to remove surplus flour. (Reserve about 1 tablespoon for sauce.)

Heat the oil in a frying pan and shallow-fry the trout (in batches) until golden brown and cooked through. Drain on kitchen paper. Arrange the fish in a single layer on a serving platter. Keep hot, without allowing to overcook.

Drain most of the oil from the pan, leaving about 1 tablespoon. Return the pan to the heat and add garlic and about 1 tablespoon of the seasoned flour. Stirring constantly, cook until the flour turns golden. Remove from the heat and pour in the vinegar, stirring constantly.

Return to stovetop over moderate heat and stir in the wine. Allow the sauce to bubble gently for 1 minute.

Pour over the fish. Serve immediately, garnished with fresh rosemary leaves and sprigs.

Serves 4 to 6

Herbed · Chicken · and · Pasta · Salad

A really delicious pasta salad, it can be served after Christmas, with leftover turkey or ham substituted for the chicken breasts. Baby green beans make a change and can be used instead of the asparagus.

Basil Vinaigrette

2 egg yolks, at room
temperature
2 tablespoons Dijon
mustard
1 cup (8 fl oz) light olive
oil

⅔ cup (5 fl oz) peanut oil
or safflower oil
¼ cup (5 fl oz) basil
vinegar (see recipe, page 72)
Freshly ground pepper
⅓ to ½ cup (2½ to 4 fl oz)
lukewarm water

Poached Chicken Breasts

2 whole (1 lb) chicken
breasts, skin removed
Cold water
1 tablespoon white wine
Salt (optional)

Freshly ground pepper
1 bay leaf
Fresh parsley
Fresh thyme

Salad

2 whole poached chicken
breasts
250 g (8 oz) snow peas,
trimmed
250 g (8 oz) young
asparagus spears

1 large red capsicum (bell
pepper), seeds and
membrane removed
500 g (1 lb) penne pasta,
cooked

1 cup (16 whole) cherry	*1 teaspoon fresh thyme leaves*
tomatoes, halved	*Salt (optional)*
⅓ cup (1 oz) shredded	*Plenty of freshly ground*
sweet basil	*black pepper*

To make the dressing: Blend the egg yolks and mustard in the bowl of a food processor. With the motor running, add the combined oils in a very steady thin trickle. Process until the mixture emulsifies. Pour in the vinegar steadily, blend in. Add salt and pepper. Set aside.

Gently poach the chicken breasts in cold water to which the white wine, salt (optional) and pepper, bay leaf, parsley sprigs and thyme sprigs have been added. Bring to a simmer, cook until chicken is tender, then leave to cool in the liquid.

Cut the chicken breasts into thick strips when they are cold and cover until required. Very lightly cook the snow peas and asparagus in boiling water. Drain well. Cut the capsicum flesh into narrow strips.

Tip the well-drained pasta into a large bowl. Add the chicken, capsicum strips, tomatoes, basil, thyme, salt and pepper. Add the dressing and mix very lightly but thoroughly. Allow to stand for about 1 hour to allow the flavours to mingle.

Just before serving, toss in the snowpeas and asparagus tips. (If snow peas and asparagus are added any length of time before serving, the dressing will cause them to lose their brightness.)

Garnish with fresh basil leaves and serve.

Serves 8

Mussels · with · Herb · Vinaigrette

To savour this dish at its very best, the mussels should be cooked and served when they are barely cold. Allow about 6 dozen mussels — or as many as you fancy!

72 mussels	*2 bay leaves*
Water	*1 tablespoon white wine*
½ teaspoon peppercorns	*vinegar*
A few parsley sprigs	*½ garlic clove, slivered*
1 thyme sprig	

Herb Vinaigrette

2 tablespoons herb vinegar   *Finely ground pepper*
(see recipe, page 73*)*   *150 ml (5 fl oz) olive oil*
2 tablespoons finely
chopped mixed herbs

Scrub the mussel shells thoroughly; discard the "beards", shreds of seaweed, etc.

Half-fill a large shallow non-reactive saucepan with water. Add the peppercorns, parsley, thyme, bay leaves, vinegar and garlic. Bring to a boil. Add the mussels, reduce the heat a little, cover the saucepan and cook ONLY until the shells open. (Discard any that do not — the shellfish is probably dead.) Set aside to cool whilst making the vinaigrette.

Pour the herb vinegar into a bowl; add the herbs and pepper. Gradually add the oil, whisking briskly all the time until well mixed and quite thick.

Remove the mussels from their shells and place them on a serving plate (they may be left in their shells, if preferred).

Serve the vinaigrette in a small bowl so diners may spoon it over their mussels. Serve with crisp salads and lots of good bread for mopping up the plates.

Serves 4

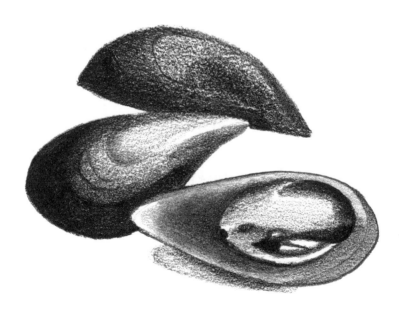

Tomato · and · Celery · Sorbet with · Basil

Serve as a palate-tingling first course on a sizzling summer day or simply as a little refresher between rather rich courses. For extra zing, a couple of drops of Tabasco sauce may be added.

6 large, very ripe tomatoes	*1 tablespoon finely*
4 tender celery stalks,	*chopped fresh basil*
coarsely chopped	*Salt*
1 to 1½ tablespoons basil	*Pepper*
vinegar (see recipe, page	*1 egg white*
72)	*Fresh basil leaves*

Blanch the tomatoes in boiling water; peel off the skins. Discard the seeds; coarsely chop the tomato flesh.

Place the tomato and celery in a blender or food processor and purée until smooth. Pour into a bowl, stir in the basil, salt and pepper.

Whisk the egg white until stiff but not dry. Gently fold into the tomato mixture.

If using an ice cream machine, pour mixture into the bowl and follow maker's instructions. To make the sorbet without a machine, a finer texture is achieved if the mixture is partially frozen in an ice cream tray BEFORE the egg white is added. When it is beginning to freeze around the edges, scoop the tomato mixture back into a bowl. Beat again and fold in the egg white. Freeze without allowing it to become rock hard!

Serve in scoops, garnished with a couple of cherry tomatoes and fresh basil leaves.

Serves 4

Kentucky · Salad

This jellied American salad is excellent with cold roast poultry or with ham. It is necessary to use canned pineapple as the enzyme action of the uncooked fruit prevents jelly from setting.

600 ml (20 fl oz) mixed	*30 g (1 oz) unflavoured*
pineapple and lemon juice	*granulated gelatine*

1 tablespoon tarragon
    vinegar (see recipe, page
    71)
2 teaspoons sugar
½ cucumber, peeled
1½ cups (5 oz) drained
    unsweetened canned

pineapple chunks (juice
    may be used as part of
    the pineapple juice
    needed in the recipe)
Lettuce leaves and mixed
    greens
Mayonnaise

Jelly

1 tablespoon gelatine

1½ to 2 cups water

Stir gelatine into very hot water until dissolved, cool to room temperature. Mix with room temperature fruit juice. Stir until sugar has dissolved. Cool.

Discard cucumber seeds, cut the flesh into small cubes. Stir in the cucumber and pineapple as the jelly begins to set.

Pour into a mold and chill until firm.

Cut into slices to serve. Arrange on the bed of mixed greens, serve mayonnaise separately.

Serves 4 to 6

Italian · Potato · Salad

Another variation of this favourite dish, this is very different from those with which most of us are familiar. Try it for a change as part of a buffet meal.

500 g (1 lb) small new
    potatoes, boiled
⅓ cup (2 oz) black olives,
    stoned
125 g (4 oz) salami
    sausage, cut into thin
    strips
2 spring onions (scallions),

cut into 2.5 cm (1 inch)
    lengths
2 small zucchini
    (courgettes), cut into
    julienne
2 tablespoons finely
    chopped parsley
2 tablespoons virgin olive oil

1 tablespoon thyme
vinegar (see recipe, page
69)
1 garlic clove, very finely
chopped

1 teaspoon fresh thyme
leaves or ½ teaspoon
dried thyme leaves
Freshly ground pepper

Cut the cooked potatoes into thin slices. Add the olives, salami, spring onions, zucchini and parsley.

Whisk together the oil, vinegar, garlic, thyme leaves and pepper.

Pour the dressing on the salad and toss well. Serve with grilled or barbecued meats. Great for a picnic.

Serves 4

NOTE: For a change, cooked long-grained rice or cooked shell pasta may be substituted for the potatoes. For an even more substantial dish, arrange quartered hard-boiled eggs on top of the salad.

Yogurt · and · Cucumber · Sauce

Similar to the Greek dip most of us know, this may also be served with vegetable crudités or with fried or grilled fish.

1 small cucumber (or about
5 Lebanese cucumbers)
1 large garlic clove, finely
chopped
1 cup (6 fl oz) natural
yogurt

1 tablespoon dill vinegar
(see recipe, page 71)
1 tablespoon chopped
fresh dill, or to taste
Pepper

Peel the cucumber; grate. Place into a colander to drain off excess liquid. (If Lebanese cucumbers are used, they need not be peeled. They may be diced rather than grated.)

Blend the cucumber and garlic into the yogurt. Add the vinegar and dill. Season with pepper to taste.

Makes about 1½ cups (8 fl oz)

NOTE: For a pleasant change, substitute Mint Vinegar (see recipe, *page 72*) and fresh mint for the dill.

Mustard · with · Green · Herbs

I love this mustard with lamb chops or cold roast lamb. It's good, too, with smoky ham or in a grilled bacon sandwich. The texture is different from most mustards, and it will "firm up" a little in the jar.

90 g (3 oz) mustard seeds
3 tablespoons dry cider
2 teaspoons finely chopped
  Italian parsley
2 teaspoons finely chopped
  chives
1½ teaspoons fresh dill or
  fennel

1½ teaspoons finely
  shredded or chopped
  salad burnet leaves
2 tablespoons tarragon vinegar
  (see recipe, page 71)
1 tablespoon clover honey,
  warmed
Salt
3 tablespoons olive oil

Place the mustard seeds, cider, herbs, vinegar, warmed honey and salt into a blender. Process until well mixed. Gradually pour in the olive oil, process until well blended.

Spoon into very small jars. Seal and use as required.

Cream · Mustard · Sauce

Serve this sauce with vegetables such as lightly cooked broccoli, asparagus, cauliflower or baby carrots. Their flavour is at its best when they are served at room temperature with this sauce. I like to use a vinegar flavoured with mixed herbs.

¼ cup (2 fl oz) herb
  vinegar (see recipe, page 73)
1 tablespoon sugar
1 tablespoon unsalted
  butter

2 teaspoons Dijon mustard
Cayenne pepper
1 egg yolk, lightly beaten
½ cup (4 fl oz) heavy
  cream

Combine the vinegar, sugar, butter, mustard and cayenne in a small saucepan; mix well. Cook over a moderately low heat, stirring constantly until lightly thickened.

Remove from the heat. Beat in the egg yolk; stir in the cream. Allow to cool to room temperature. Serve as suggested.

Makes about ¾ cup (6 fl oz)

Floral Vinegars

For centuries, herbalists have experimented with flowers in food, liqueurs and medicine. A quick glance through an old herbal offers some pretty hair-raising "cures". It is surprising to see which herbs and flowers were once accepted as edible, if not palatable.

With the new spirit of adventure in food presentation, flowers have gradually started to reappear on plates — first appearing as a pretty garnish, then as an ingredient. Flowers are also appearing again in vinegar bottles, with delicious results.

When making floral vinegars it's essential to choose flowers that are not harmful and that have a pleasant taste. Herb flowers are the obvious choice, but roses, lavender, violets, marigolds, nasturtiums, carnations, primroses and elderflowers are also excellent. Make sure the petals are not harbouring any little creepy-crawlies! Fine quality white wine vinegar will provide the perfect base, and a touch of honey will sweeten and enhance the flavour.

Use about three-quarters of a cup of flower heads to two cups (16 fl oz) of vinegar. Half-fill a jar with the clean, dry flowers, then top them up with vinegar and seal the jar. Allow it to stand in a sunny spot for about two weeks. Check for flavour: if weak, leave longer, otherwise strain and bottle. Add one flower to the vinegar for garnish and identification.

Another method involves heating the vinegar first, then pouring it over the flowers. Seal the jar and allow the flowers to steep for two days, then strain and bottle the liquid.

You can delight a friend with a gift of a pretty basket filled with a jar of lavender honey, a bottle of lavender vinegar, lavender biscuits (any crisp, buttery biscuit recipe will do — just add a couple of tablespoons of crumbled dried lavender flowers to the mixture) and a bunch of fresh lavender tied with a lavender satin ribbon. And the bonus is that you will have as much pleasure creating these delectables as you will have in giving them!

A · Vinegar · of · Roses · and · Raspberries

I love to experiment with different vinegar flavours and this has become one of my favourites. Rosy and fragrant, the promise of summer delight wafts from the bottle as it is unstoppered. Use it in a dressing to serve with fruit salads, cold duck breast or as a cordial base for a long drink, with a little sugar syrup added.

1 cup (2 oz) dark red rose petals
½ cup (2 oz) ripe raspberries

5 to 6 cups (40 to 50 fl oz) white wine vinegar

Place the rose petals into a bowl, gently crushing them. Add the raspberries, crushing them a little. Pour on the vinegar and stir well. Transfer to a wide-necked jar, cover with a glass, ceramic or plastic lid.

Stand the jar on a sunny window ledge for a couple of weeks. Strain the vinegar very well using muslin or very fine nylon.

Pour into bottles, add a couple of rose petals — if you like — and cork or stopper.

Makes about 5 to 6 cups (40 to 50 fl oz)

NOTE: For a different and distinctive flavour, add a cinnamon stick, but do not leave it there for more than about 3 days as its flavour develops very quickly.

Fragrant · Rubbing · Lotion

Pleasant and refreshing for anyone confined to bed for any length of time, this is much more enjoyable as a rub than methylated spirits. Use herbs such as lemon verbena, rosemary, lavender, mint, scented geranium leaves, dark red rose petals or violets.

600 ml (20 fl oz) mild   *A good handful of*
white wine vinegar   *preferred herbs or floral*
         petals

Place the crushed herbs or flowers into a jar; pour on the vinegar. Allow to stand for 2 or 3 weeks, shaking the jar occasionally.

Strain and pour into pretty bottles.

I make no promises, mind you, but my mother used to soak a brown paper strip in a herbal vinegar and wrap it around her brow to ease a bad headache!

Makes about 600 ml (20 fl oz)

Rose · Geranium · Jelly

This very beautiful jelly is superb with hot or cold roast lamb, poultry or veal.

A handful of rose   *1 teaspoon allspice berries*
geranium leaves, washed   *4 cups (32 fl oz) water*
1 to 2 tablespoons vinegar   *125 g (4 oz) powdered*
of roses and raspberries   *pectin*
(see recipe, page 87)   *A few drops red food*
5 cups (40 oz) sugar   *colouring, if desired*

Gently crush the rose geranium leaves. Place them in a large ceramic, glass or stainless steel bowl; add the vinegar. Tip in the sugar; mix in the allspice berries. Allow to stand for at least 2 hours.

Place the mixture into a large non-reactive saucepan. Add the water and bring to a boil. Simmer for a couple of minutes. Allow to cool completely before straining.

Add the pectin. Bring to a boil again and cook vigorously for about 1 minute.

Remove from the heat and add food colouring, if using.

Pour into small sterilised jars. Add a rose geranium leaf or a red rose petal to each. Seal the jars. If an opened jar is not used at one time, refrigerate any remaining jelly.

Makes about ten 90 to 125 g (3 to 4 oz) jars

Fruit Vinegars

Making fruit vinegar is an old pantry tradition that has been neglected too long. They are easy to make and allow us to enjoy the fragrance and flavour of luscious summer fruits all year.

Originally fruit vinegars were used as cordials, either warmed with a spoon of honey to soothe sore throats, or served with cold water, ice and sugar syrup, as a refreshing drink on a hot summer's day. They are delicious as a cordial made with soda or sparkling mineral water and a twist of orange or lemon peel.

Peaches, plums, cherries and apricots are all suitable for fruit vinegars, but perhaps the best of all are based on berries: raspberries, blackberries, mulberries, lightly crushed blueberries, and black and red currants are all wonderful. If the fruit remains too long in the jar of vinegar it will become cloudy as the fruit disintegrates, but the flavour will be intense. If appearance is important, strain it several times through very fine muslin.

You can also make vinegar from fruit wine. In the 19th century and early this century, many country housewives made their own wines and vinegars from fruits such as gooseberries.

You can sprinkle fruit vinegars on fruit salads and use them in dressings, and they make a delicious marinade or basting solution for meats — try raspberry with lamb, plum with pork, and cherry with duck.

Fermented · Raspberry · Vinegar

I found this recipe in an old English cookbook and experimented with it last summer. Apart from the excitement of having the occasional cork pop out, it was most successful and I have only recently used the last of it as a delicious cordial. I'm eagerly awaiting this summer's berry crops to make another batch and to experiment with other berries.

1 kg (2 lb) ripe raspberries	*Boiling water*
500 g (1 lb) white sugar	*1 teaspoon brewer's yeast,*
1 l (32 fl oz) white wine	*or 1 tablespoon sultanas*
vinegar	

Pick over the fruit carefully, discarding any fruits showing mildew traces. (This will spoil the vinegar.) Remove hulls. Place the berries into a large china glass bowl.

Dissolve the sugar in the vinegar. Pour the mixture over the fruit. Stir well, using a wooden spoon. Cover with a teatowel and allow to stand for 2 days.

Strain the liquid through muslin, pressing the fruit to extract as much juice as possible. Place the berry pulp into a bowl, pour on sufficient boiling water to barely cover the pulp. Stir well and let stand until cold. Strain through a muslin cloth, squeezing well to extract as much liquid as possible. Mix this liquid into a vinegar mixture and discard the pulp.

Add the yeast (if using) or sultanas; cover loosely. Allow the mixture to bubble away and when it has ceased its seething, strain it into bottles and cork firmly.

Makes about 5 to 6 cups (40 to 48 fl oz)

Raspberry · Vinegar
(Sweetened)

This is the sour-sweet raspberry vinegar I remember from my childhood. Filtered sunlight through old trees, dolly tea-parties and little glasses of home-made raspberry vinegar sipped through deliciously puckered lips — one mouthful and I am transported back to those early days. Quite different from the sharp raspberry vinegar we use in some of our other recipes in this book, this is well worth making for the touch of nostalgia it inspires.

1 kg (2 lb) ripe raspberries   500 g (1 lb) granulated
500 ml (16 fl oz) white   sugar to each 600 ml
   wine vinegar   (16 fl oz) of juice

In a china or glass bowl, combine the raspberries and the vinegar. Allow to steep for at least 24 hours. Press out the juices from the fruit. Strain through muslin. Add sugar to juice.

Pour into a large non-reactive saucepan. Cook, stirring often, over moderate heat until the sugar dissolves. Bring to a boil and simmer until the mixture reaches a syrupy consistency.

Makes about 4 cups (32 fl oz)

NOTE: If you press the fruit while the juice is draining through, you will get more juice but the syrup will be cloudy rather than ruby-clear.

Black · Currant · Vinegar

This is another vinegar to be served as a drink, although I like to add some to cooked fruits, fresh berries, salad dressing and use it in various other ways. Only for those lucky enough to have bountiful supplies of those wonderful black currants.

2½ kg (5 lb) black currants　　*270 g (9 oz) sugar to each*
1 l (32 fl oz) best-quality　　　*500 ml (16 fl oz) of juice*
white wine vinegar

Mash the fruit into a large china bowl. Pour in the vinegar and stir. Allow to stand for 24 to 36 hours.

Strain through a jelly-bag, muslin or cheesecloth. (I use an old well-boiled nylon curtain!) Allow to drain slowly for up to 24 hours.

Measure the juice. Add the appropriate amount of sugar and place into a non-reactive preserving pan or large saucepan. Bring to a boil. Allow to simmer for about 15 minutes. Bottle for future use.

Makes about 6 cups (48 fl oz)

Pineapple · Vinegar
(Home-made)

Create this "personalised" vinegar in your own kitchen. I keep mine in a large clip top preserving jar and share the occasional glass of white wine with it — this enhances the flavour and mellows the vinegar.

Peel of ½ pineapple　　　*1 slice of pineapple*
¼ cup (1½ oz) brown dark　*2 l (8 cups) water*
sugar

Place all of the ingredients into a large jar and stir well. Cover with plastic. Set in sunlight.

When the mixture begins to ferment, remove half of the peel. As the liquid changes colour and becomes acid to the taste, remove the rest of the peel and flesh. It will then become a very pale colour and very acidic. This takes about 2½ weeks.

Strain and store. Use in dressings, etc. to add an interesting and different tang to a dish.

Makes about 8 cups (64 fl oz)

Peach · Vinegar

Use this summer fragrant vinegar to splash on luscious, lightly-sugared strawberries or use as a dressing on a chicken salad served with thickly sliced, fresh, yellow peaches.

3 yellow peaches, peeled   *600 ml (20 fl oz) white*
   and quartered   *wine vinegar*
3 whole cloves

Prepare the peaches, press the cloves into the peach pieces.

Place the peaches into a wide-mouthed jar and pour on the slightly warmed vinegar. Cover tightly and allow to stand for 2 weeks before straining the vinegar from the peaches. Pour the vinegar into bottles; seal and use as required.

The tangy peach segments may be served with cold meats.

Makes 600 ml (20 fl oz)

Cherry · Vinegar

Capture the flavour of cherries during their short season and enjoy this fragrant vinegar during the cold days of winter. Use to deglaze a pan used for cooking steaks or as the base for a tangy sauce to serve with duck and other rich meats.

1 cup dark cherries   *600 ml (20 fl oz) white or*
1 tablespoon sugar   *red wine vinegar*

Rinse the cherries, then place them into a wide-mouthed jar; add the sugar. Pour on the warmed vinegar, seal and allow to stand for at least 12 days before straining and bottling.

Makes 600 ml (20 fl oz)

Blackberry · Vinegar

500 g (1 lb) blackberries   500 g (1 lb) sugar
500 ml (16 fl oz) white   1 cup (10 oz) honey
   wine vinegar

Put blackberries and vinegar into a jar with a plastic lid, cover and leave in a cupboard for one week, giving the jar a shake every day. Strain into a saucepan. Add sugar and honey, stir and bring slowly to the boil. Simmer for 10 minutes.
   Cool and bottle.

Makes about 2 to 3 cups (16 to 24 fl oz)

South · American · Chicory · and Nectarine · Salad

This recipe was brought back by a friend who spent some time in South America. If you find chicory too bitter, substitute small cos lettuce leaves with perhaps just a little curly endive to give a sharp edge to the flavour.

2 cups (4 oz) chicory   1 ripe tomato, cut into thin
   leaves, torn, washed and   wedges
   dried well   2 ripe nectarines, each cut
1 cup (4 oz) mung bean   into 8 wedges
   sprouts or cress   1 tablespoon orange juice
                              Red onion rings, for garnish

Dressing

¼ cup (2 fl oz) raspberry   3 tablespoons hazelnut oil
   vinegar (see recipe, page   White pepper
   91)

To make the dressing mix together the raspberry vinegar, hazelnut oil and pepper.
   Toss the chicory and bean shoots with half of the dressing. Arrange on an attractive platter. Top with the tomato wedges.
   Mix together the nectarine slices and orange juice. Arrange on top of the tomatoes; garnish with the onion rings.
   Drizzle with the remaining dressing. Serve at once.
   Excellent with cold poultry or ham.

Serves 4

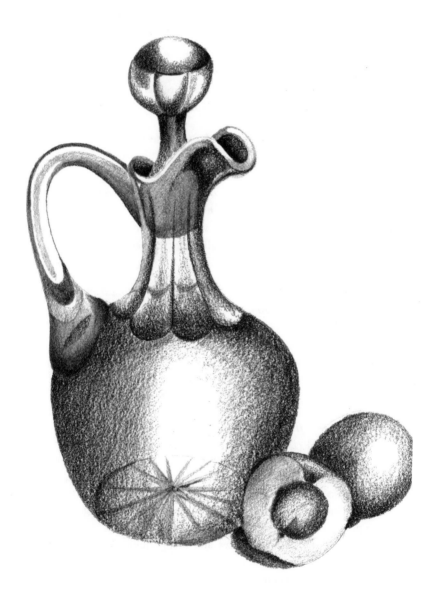

Warm · Chicken · Salad · with Raspberry · Vinegar

This combination of flavours is a legacy from the trendy days of "nouvelle cuisine", but it really is very good and a lovely choice for a luncheon.

2 skinless chicken breast fillets	vinegar (see recipe, page 91)
12 baby spinach leaves	½ tablespoon white wine vinegar
3 tablespoons olive oil	1 cup (2 oz) small lettuce leaves, torn
3 tablespoons pine nuts	
1½ tablespoons rasberry	Pepper

Cut the chicken into fine strips. Wash and dry spinach leaves, discarding any hard stalks.

Heat 2 tablespoons of the olive oil in a skillet. Stir-fry the chicken for several minutes. Add the spinach and cook for about 1 minute, or until barely wilted.

Add the pine nuts and cook for 1 more minute. Spoon the contents of the pan onto serving plates. Pour the vinegars into the pan with the remaining 1 tablespoon of oil. Season with pepper and stir until mixed. Lightly toss with the torn lettuce leaves.

Pour over the salad on the plates and serve immediately.

Serves 2

Middle · Eastern · Potato · Salad

Quite different from the familiar potato salad our mothers served, the unexpected addition of raspberry vinegar creates a sharp and interesting flavour variation in this dish. If you don't enjoy the flavour of raspberry vinegar, substitute cider vinegar.

4 medium potatoes, unpeeled	chopped fresh parsley
2 tablespoons raspberry vinegar (see recipe, page 91) or cider vinegar	3 spring onions (scallions), chopped
2 tablespoons peanut oil	1 tablespoon chopped fresh dill
1 tablespoon lemon juice	2 tablespoons finely chopped fresh mint
1 garlic clove, crushed or very finely chopped	Pepper to taste
⅓ cup (1 handful) finely	Paprika

Cook the potatoes in gently boiling water for about 20 minutes, or until tender. Drain but do not peel.

Dice as soon as cool enough to handle and place in a glass or ceramic bowl. Add the vinegar, oil, lemon juice and garlic. Mix lightly and allow to cool.

When the potatoes are cool, toss in the parsley, onions, dill, mint and pepper. Serve at room temperature, sprinkled with a little paprika.

Serves 4

NOTE: Dill flavoured vinegar offers a pleasant change (see recipe, *page 71*).

Jellied · Tomato · Ring · with · Basil

Wonderfully refreshing to the palate for a summer luncheon, garnish the mold with fresh basil leaves and summer-flowering herb blossoms.

2 cups (16 fl oz) tomato juice	2 tablespoons raspberry vinegar (see recipe, page 91) or basil vinegar (see recipe, page 72)
250 g (8 oz) sliced ripe tomatoes	
1 small onion, chopped	2 envelopes unflavoured gelatine
1 bay leaf	
6 black peppercorns	Fresh basil leaves, for garnish
2 whole cloves (optional)	
2 tablespoons dry white wine	Herb flowers (such as borage, thyme, mint, dill etc.)

Set aside 1 cup (8 fl oz) of the tomato juice, the gelatine, herb sprigs and flowers. Combine all of the other ingredients in a non-reactive saucepan. Bring to the boil. Reduce the heat and simmer for 5 minutes.

Remove the spices. Pour the tomato juice mixture into a blender or food processor. Blend until smooth. Sprinkle the gelatine on the hot mixture and stir until dissolved. (If preferred, dissolve first in a little very hot water.)

Stir in the reserved 1 cup (8 fl oz) of tomato juice and pour into a mold or ring tin. Chill until firm. Unmold and serve the ring with the centre filled with herb sprigs and garnished with herb flowers. A handful of little cherry tomatoes may be popped into the hollow of the jelly ring.

Serves 6 to 8

Spiced Vinegar

Most vinegars are a suitable base for spiced vinegar, with cider and white wine vinegars offering a milder flavour than malt vinegar. The colourless cider and white wine vinegars also give a better appearance to preserved vegetables. However, in robust sauces, chutneys and some pickles, malt vinegar is quite satisfactory.

For pickling it is better to use a commercial vinegar, which has its acetic acid level indicated on the label, rather than one made at home with an indeterminate acetic acid level. For safe and successful pickles look for a level of at least four percent. And do not boil vigorously for too long or the acetic acid will lose its strength and effectiveness for pickling.

Traditionally the spices for vinegar are tied in small squares of muslin and dangled into the vinegar from the rim of a non-reactive saucepan; this enables them to be easily removed. But I find it equally effective to add them loose, and to strain them later. Either way, add spices to the vinegar, bring to a boil, hold there for a few minutes, then remove the vinegar from the heat, allowing the spices to remain in the vinegar for a couple of hours before removing. You can use the vinegar immediately for pickling or store it in bottles or jars, with vinegar-proof covers, until required. When pickling vegetables that have a crisp texture use a cold vinegar solution to maintain the crispness. I like to cover the vinegar with melted wax to prolong shelf-life before sealing with a non-metallic lid.

And don't throw out the vinegar solution left over from pickles. It's useful for dips, sauces and salad dressings.

Spiced · Vinegar

Apart from providing a useful base for pickles, relishes and chutneys, a dash of spiced vinegar may be added to casseroles or pea soup.

1 l (32 fl oz) white wine vinegar	2.5 cm (1 inch) piece green ginger, chopped
1½ teaspoons black peppercorns	1 small cinnamon stick
1 teaspoon celery seeds	1 small red chili (optional)
1 teaspoon mustard seeds	2 teaspoons sugar
½ teaspoon whole cloves	

Pour the vinegar into a large non-reactive saucepan and add all the remaining ingredients. Stir until well mixed.

Bring to a boil. Simmer for 5 minutes. Cool and bottle without straining, although I like to remove the cinnamon stick, which does develop a very strong flavour.

Makes about 4 cups (32 fl oz)

Chili · Vinegar

Fierce little red chilies add the heat to this vinegar — and it is important to remember to thoroughly wash your hands after dealing with them. You can control the fieriness of the vinegar by the number of chilies used and also by leaving or discarding the seeds, which are *really* hot!

600 ml (20 fl oz) white
wine vinegar
5 to 6 little red chilies

A few shreds of lemon zest
(optional)

If whole chilies are to be used, simply put them into a bottle, top with the vinegar of your choice, and add a few shreds of lemon peel. Seal bottles and store in a dark cupboard.

Makes about 600 ml (20 fl oz)

Spicy · Chicken

Tangy and delicious, this dish is very good served with pasta. I like to make several batches and freeze some for future use — a great standby to have tucked away!

4 chicken pieces, skin
removed
30 g (1 oz) butter
1 tablespoon olive oil
2 large onions, finely
chopped
1 green capsicum (bell
pepper), seeds and
membranes removed and
flesh diced
1 garlic clove, finely chopped

2 tablespoons tomato purée
2 teaspoons dry mustard
300 ml (10 fl oz) chicken
stock
2 tablespoons (1 oz)
brown sugar
3 tablespoons spiced vinegar
(see recipe, page 100)
1 teaspoon Worcestershire
sauce
Freshly ground black pepper

Prepare the chicken joints. Heat the butter and oil in a heavy pan. Brown chicken joints on all sides; transfer to a casserole.

Lightly sauté the onions, capsicum and garlic. Add to chicken in the casserole.

Stir together the tomato purée and mustard. Add to the stock, sugar, vinegar, worcestershire sauce and pepper. Mix well, stirring until the sugar dissolves. Pour over the chicken.

Cover the casserole and cook in a preheated 160°C (225°F) oven for about 1¼ hours, or until the chicken pieces are tender.

Serves 4

Savoury · Liver

Although spiced vinegar is most often used for pickling or preserving, it may also be used to add piquancy to savoury dishes.

500 g (1 lb) lamb's fry or
calf liver
Seasoned flour, for coating
Oil, for frying
2 garlic cloves, finely
chopped
1 teaspoon chopped fresh

oregano or marjoram, or
½ teaspoon dried
oregano
¼ cup (2 fl oz) spiced
vinegar (see recipe, page
100)
¼ cup (2 fl oz) dry white wine

Remove the skin and tubes from the liver and discard; thinly slice the liver. Pat dry. Dip each slice into lightly seasoned flour.

Heat the oil and shallow-fry on each side until browned and lightly cooked. Place the liver in a serving dish and keep hot.

Drain off most of the oil from the pan. Add the garlic and oregano and sprinkle in a little flour. Stir over moderate heat for 1 to 2 minutes.

Remove from the heat and let cool a little. Pour in the vinegar. Return to the heat, add the wine and cook, stirring constantly, for 2 minutes.

Pour the sauce over the liver.

Cover and allow to stand for a few minutes before serving.

Serves 4

Mixed · Vegetable · Pickles

A lovely addition to any buffet spread or to serve with a simple meal of breads, cheese and cold meats, make this pickle when summer vegetables are at their best and cheapest.

3 tablespoons coarse salt
5 cups (40 fl oz) water
½ small cauliflower
4 small zucchini
(courgettes)

1 green capsicum (bell
pepper)
1 red capsicum (bell pepper)
2 green tomatoes (if
available)

2 small carrots
1 celery stalk
2 garlic cloves, slivered
1 small chili pepper, seeds
    discarded

Fresh thyme sprigs
Fresh or dried bay leaves
4 cups (32 fl oz) spiced
    vinegar (see recipe, page
    100)

Stir the salt into the water. Bring to a boil; set aside until cooked.

Wash the vegetables; pat dry. Cut the cauliflower into small florets. Cut the zucchini into thick diagonal slices. Discard the membranes and seeds from the capsicum and cut into strips or slices.

Peel the carrots and cut lengthwise into eights. Cut in half. (Cook in boiling water for 3 to 4 minutes, if carrots appear a little woody.)

Cut the celery into 5 cm (2 inch) lengths. Cut each tomato into 8 wedges.

Place all of the vegetables into a large bowl and cover with the cold brine solution. Allow to stand for at least 24 hours. Rinse under cold running water and drain very well.

Pack into sterilised preserving jars. Add garlic slivers and a shred or two of chili. (Wash hands carefully after handling these fiery little devils!) Tuck a thyme sprig and a bay leaf into each jar.

Bring the spiced vinegar to a boil. Pour over the vegetables. Seal and allow to stand for several weeks before serving.

Makes about four 250 g (8 oz) jars

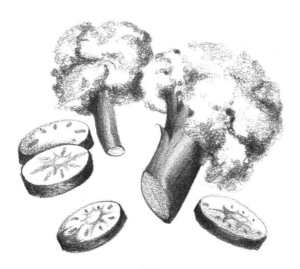

Pickled · Aubergine
(Eggplant)

Look for the pale-coloured long aubergines that sometimes appear in our greengrocers — they are excellent for this recipe. If they are unavailable, choose aubergines that are as small, light coloured and as unblemished as possible.

1 kg (2 lb) small
aubergines (eggplants)
3 garlic cloves, slivered
2 celery stalks with leaves,
cut into thick slices and
leaves chopped
1 red capsicum (bell
pepper), cut into thick
strips

1 white onion, thinly sliced
from tip to root
2 tablespoons finely
chopped parsley
Sprigs of wild fennel* or
dill
Bay leaves
4 cups (32 fl oz) spiced
vinegar (see recipe, page
100)

Remove and discard the stems from the aubergines. Pierce each aubergine with a small sharp-pointed knife. Bring salted water to a boil, plunge in the aubergines and bring the water back to a boil. Remove from the heat. Cover the saucepan and let stand for 5 minutes. Drain well. Cut into quarters, if small; otherwise, thickly slice.

Toss the vegetables and garlic with the choppd parsley and pack into sterilised jars. Add a sprig of fennel or dill and a bay leaf to each jar.

Bring the spiced vinegar to a boil. Strain and pour over the vegetables. Seal and store for at least 2 weeks before serving.

*Wild fennel is that feathery, anise-scented "weed" that grows in neglected paddocks and beside railway tracks. It is readily identifiable by its lacy golden flowers. I rather like to add just a few seeds from the mature flowerheads to the pickle, if available, otherwise use a flowerhead!

Makes about three 250 g (8 oz) jars

Pickled · Crab · Apples

I envy those people who have laden crab apple trees and cherish those crab apples that generous friends give me. This simple recipe is well worth making, and you will enjoy these pickled fruits with cold meats and poultry, or with a tasty cheese.

1 kg (2 lb) ripe but firm
crab apples
4 cups (32 fl oz) spiced
vinegar (see recipe, page
100)
¾ cup (6 oz) granulated
sugar

½ teaspoon salt
1 small piece of cinnamon
stick
2 whole cloves
Thinly peeled rind of ¼
orange

Trim the crab apple stem, leaving about 1.2 cm (½ inch) on the apples. Bring the spiced vinegar to a boil. Add the sugar, salt, cinnamon stick and cloves.

Place the crab apples in the vinegar and simmer for no more than 10 minutes. Stir gently once or twice during the cooking time.

Spoon the crab apples into jars. Pour over the strained spiced vinegar. Seal tightly.

To keep the apples for a long period, it is necessary to use a preserving outfit, but these will keep very well under refrigeration for many weeks.

Makes about four 250g (8 fl oz) jars

Cheddar · Cheese · with · Walnuts

This zesty cheese makes an excellent gift. Spoon it into small attractive crockery pots and accompany it with a spatula for spreading and a recipe for this very tasty spread.

250 g (8 oz) grated tasty
(Sharp or Jack) cheese
90 g (3 oz) butter, softened
½ teaspoon Dijon mustard
1 tablespoon chili vinegar
(see recipe, page 100)

⅓ cup (1 oz) very finely
chopped walnuts
Good pinch of cayenne
pepper

Very finely grate the cheese. Mix in the butter until well blended.

Stir together the mustard and vinegar; mix into the cheese mixture. Add the walnuts and cayenne, mixing to ensure they are evenly distributed through the cheese.

Spoon the cheese mixture into small crocks or jars. Cover with a little softened butter or a thin layer of olive oil or walnut oil. Store in the refrigerator but allow to come to room temperature before serving.

Makes 2 small crocks or jars

Distilled and Spirit Vinegars

Distilled and spirit vinegars are used mainly in the commercial manufacture of pickles and sauces.

Any vinegar can be distilled, but malt vinegars are generally used. The flavour, however, is less pungent than malt vinegar, and it is useful when a mild pickle is required. It is colourless and good for pickling red cabbage, cucumber and beans etc.

Spirit vinegars have a high acetic acid content (10 to 13 percent) and an extremely sharp taste. Molasses is fermented and distilled before all the alcohol has been converted to acetic acid, so a residue of alcohol remains. It is colourless and is used mainly for commercial pickling. Spirit vinegars are normally available in shops.

Hungarian · Braised · Beef

Hearty and appetising for a winter dinner, this may be served to a hungry family or to dinner party guests.

2 tablespoons peanut or
   vegetable oil
1½ kg (3¾ lb) beef brisket,
   trimmed of fat
Salt (optional)
Freshly ground pepper
3 onions, each cut into 8
   segments
1 cup (8 fl oz) light ale
   (beer)
2 cups (16 fl oz) water
1½ tablespoons distilled
   white vinegar

2 tablespoons sweet
   paprika, or to taste
6 parsley sprigs
500 g (1 lb) potatoes,
   peeled and halved
2 teaspoons cornflour
   (cornstarch) dissolved in
   2 tablespoons cold water
⅓ cup (2½ fl oz) heavy
   cultured sour cream
Lemon juice, to taste
Chopped parsley

Heat the oil in an ovenproof casserole just large enough to hold the brisket and potatoes. Add the meat and brown on all sides. Remove to a plate and keep warm; sprinkle with salt and pepper.

Add the onions to the pan and cook over moderately low heat until softened but not coloured.

Add the beer, water, vinegar, paprika, parsley sprigs and salt and pepper to taste. Bring to a boil. Return the meat to the casserole.

Cover the casserole and roast in a preheated 160°C (325°F) oven for 2½ to 3 hours, until the meat is tender when pierced with a fork. (Flavour and tenderness depend upon slow cooking of the meat.)

While the meat cooks, parboil the potatoes. Add to the casserole during the last 30 minutes of cooking.

When the meat and potatoes are tender, transfer to a serving platter and keep warm. Discard the parsley sprigs; skim all fat from the surface of the cooking liquid. Put liquid and solids through a food mill or sieve, or purée it in a food processor. Pour in a large saucepan and cook over moderately high heat until reduced to about 2 cups. Whisk in the cornflour/water mixture and simmer for a couple of minutes. Whisk in the sour cream, lemon juice and salt and pepper to taste. Gently reheat. Slice the meat across the grain and serve with sour cream.

Serves 6

Preserved · Figs

For me, one of the real delights of summer is being able to enjoy the lusciousness of sun-ripened figs — but they are with us for such a short time! Make this wonderful preserve and enjoy figs, albeit figs with a different flavour, throughout the four seasons.

3 kg (6¾ lb) white   *2 cups (16 fl oz) distilled*
(granulated) sugar   *white vinegar*
2 cups (16 fl oz) water   *3 kg (6¾ lb) firm, ripe figs*

Place the sugar, water and vinegar into a large non-reactive saucepan or preserving pan. Simmer gently, stirring often, until the sugar dissolves. Cook for 10 minutes over medium heat.

Remove the stems and peels (if they slip off readily) from the figs, leaving the fruit intact. Add the figs to the syrup and simmer very gently over low heat for about 4 hours, or until the figs are a translucent russet-gold colour.

Spoon gently into hot, sterilised jars; allow to cool completely before sealing.

Although they are perfect with cold meats, such as ham, boiled corned beef, tongue, etc., I love these figs served icy cold with crème fraîche or natural yogurt, well sprinkled with cinnamon and finely grated orange and lemon rind.

Makes about three 500 ml (16 fl oz) jars

Index

INDEX

Wontons with dipping sauce,
vegetarian 42
Worcestershire sauce, Kate Murphy's
39

Yogurt and cucumber sauce 84

Zucchini
Italian potato salad 83
mixed vegetable pickles 102
spring vegetable terrine with
champagne dressing 31
vegetarian wontons 42